R

ON THE RADIO

Ryan
ON THE RADIO

Paul Russell

**GILL AND MACMILLAN
AND
RADIO TELIFÍS ÉIREANN**

Published by
Gill and Macmillan Ltd
Goldenbridge
Dublin 8
and
Radio Telefís Éireann
Donnybrook
Dublin 4
with associated companies in
Auckland, Delhi, Gaborone, Hamburg, Harare,
Hong Kong, Johannesburg, Kuala Lumpur, Lagos, London,
Manzini, Melbourne, Mexico City, Nairobi,
New York, Singapore, Tokyo
Text © Paul Russell 1991
Illustrations © Jim Walpole and Martin Maher
0 7171 1917 3
Design by Fergus O'Keeffe, Dublin
Typesetting by
Seton Music Graphics Ltd, Co. Cork
Printed by
Colour Books Ltd, Dublin

*Thanks to Noel Gavin and the Star Newspaper for
permission to reproduce photographs*

Contents

Acknowledgments

This book would have remained a flash in the frying pan of brilliant ideas for bar-room discussion only, were it not for a few decent human beings.

Most human of them all is *The Ryan Show* team, both past and present. For the ease of access to the world of Ryan, I would like to say sincere thanks to: Gerry Ryan, Siobhain 'Miles of Files' Hough, Joan Torsney, Willy O'Reilly, Pat Dunne, Brenda Donohue, Barbara Jordan, Maggie Stapleton and Nita Byrne.

Special thanks to Cathal McCabe and Bill O'Donovan. Thanks also to Michael Croke.

To Brendan Farrelly and Helen Rogers — thank you for dragging me through the slime and cleaning up my act, page by page.

I would also like to thank Noel Gavin and the *Star* newspaper for their valuable help.

To Linz — thank you for keeping me on the skateboard.

And finally, thanks to my editor, Fergal Tobin, for giving me an impossible deadline and having a sense of humour.

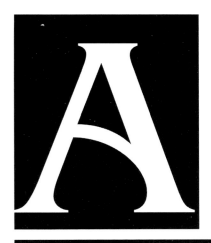

A day....

The early morning runs for cover

The early morning runs for cover as the 'Houghmobile' roars into the car park at 2FM. It's 7.30 a.m. Bang on time with an hour and a half to go to Ryan on the radio. As the first of the team to arrive, Siobhain Hough sets the hectic pace of a new day by buying the newspapers and sweet-talking a couple of tea bags from Ian Dempsey and the *Breakfast Show* crew who have been on the air since 7 a.m. She never fails.

There's a long list of calls on the answering machine that have come into the office overnight. There's some early post, left in by hand, amongst which is a plea for help from a woman who's got green goo on her new carpet and can't get it removed.

'Yep,' thinks Siobhain. 'That's definitely one for the show.'

As the rush hour starts to build in the city, producer Joan Torsney jogs into the office. She's the show's health expert and is always on cue to point out how many horrible things there are in a cream bun.

'Is Gerry not in yet?' she asks Siobhain.

'No. Maybe I should give him a call. He might have slept it out.'

'No. Let's give him a few more minutes,' says Joan as she dunks a tea bag.

It's 8.15. Less than an hour to go to the show. And Terence is in a bit of a fluster on the line from Cork.

'Hi, Siobhain. Can I talk to Gerry?'

1

'We'd all like to talk to Gerry, Terence. But he's not in yet. D'you want to give him a call when he's on the air. You won't miss him then,' says Siobhain.

An army of tourists on roller skates

'Oh, I might all right,' he replies in that cunning Cork tone. 'I've somethin' to tell him.'

'What is it?' she asks.

'Oh, I'm not tellin' ya. You'll only laugh,' he titters and hangs up.

A noise like the sound of an army of tourists on roller skates comes howling into the office. But no one pays any heed. It's only Brenda and Barbara. For the last couple of days they've been racing each other into the building. And whoever comes second gets 'the sewer job', a grim title for a report on the show that might be a little uncomfortable to do – like reporting from an underground sewerage tunnel. This time Brenda's the loser. Barbara raises her arms in the air like a true champ.

'No offence, Brenda,' Barbara laughs. 'But you're a bit out of shape.'

'The day's only started, Barbara,' Brenda smiles. 'I'll get you back.'

By 8.30 Siobhain has copies of the show's running order for everyone. This gives the details and approximate times of any items that have been arranged for the day's show, such as guest interviews, competitions and phonecalls.

2

But there's still no sign of Gerry. Siobhain phones home. There's no reply.

'Where is he?' she asks out loud.

The last of the team to arrive is producer Paul Russell. He heads straight for Siobhain, not to discuss the running order but to talk about the contents of last night's *Coronation Street*.

'Hey, d'ya see the story in the paper about the snake they found in this girl's stomach?' Joan asks. 'It was there, growing inside her for six months. God, it must be enormous. Yeuk!'

The door bursts open

'Great!' says Paul. 'Let's start with that on the show this morning. Just the thing after breakfast.'

 At 8.45 the studio is ready and waiting. All the studios in the radio building are located downstairs from the office. Next to Gerry's studio, through a thick glass window, Ian Dempsey is getting a traffic report on *The Breakfast Show*.

The heating in Gerry's studio isn't working. 'I bet you he'll say something about that on air. I bet you!' says Siobhain.

'Yeah. If he gets here to say it at all. Where is he?' Joan replies.

Three minutes to go. Ian wraps up his show and introduces the news at nine. The phone lines are switched over to *The Ryan Show*: 2830222. Already there's been an angry caller on to the show complaining about not being able to get tickets for the next soccer international.

Paul leans into Ian's studio and asks him to hang on at his desk.

'You may have another show to do. Gerry's not in.'

'And the weather . . .' the newsreader announces, meaning that if Gerry's not in the studio in ten seconds all hell will break loose.

'Sorry. Didn't have enough money for the toll bridge. I nearly had to turn back,' says Gerry as he dashes over to his seat, shoves his headphones on, switches on the red light and it's . . .

'Ryan on the radio from now till midday. I'm a little out of breath but I'll tell you all about that after the first record. God, it's freezing in here this morning.' He looks out at the control room. 'Siobhain,' he shouts for all the nation to hear. 'Is the heater working?'

'I told you,' Siobhain laughs. 'I knew he'd say something. I just knew it.' And another show is ceremoniously launched.

Each day of the programme the studio is operated by just four people. There's Gerry, there's one producer and two broadcasting assistants, or BAs. It is the BAs who answer the many hundreds of phone calls that come in to the show every morning. The calls are the life blood of *The Gerry Ryan Show*. It's the variety of stories, opinions and thoughts from callers that makes *The GR Show* bounce along day after day.

Siobhain and Nita answer those calls.

Gerry loves to talk The producer decides the shape of the show, steers the topic and discussions in the right direction so as not to let it get too one-sided or repetitive. The response of the listeners also helps decide where the show goes. The calls are live.There is no device to delay their comments. It's this risk that gives the programme that extra edge. And then there's Gerry. Plugged in and switched on, he carries the full weight of the show, never knowing what the next caller is going to say, never knowing where the conversation's going to go next.

Siobhain Hough, pictured in the control room taking calls for the show. In the studio, left to right: Joan, Nita, Gerry.

In front of him is the studio desk with a variety of controls and equipment. With the flick of a fader he can operate the record decks, the CD players, the tape decks, microphones for his guests and the all-important telephone lines. There are three lines into the studio so at any one time Gerry could be talking to three people on the phone and a guest or two in the studio.

4

Studio

●●●●●●●●●●●●●●●●●●●●●●●●●●●●●●●●●●●●●●●

At the centre of every broadcast is the studio. And every morning as the show progresses through its three-hour run the small room underneath the station's offices takes on a life of its own. That has nothing to do with the voltage or the hum of hi-tech machines running through its veins. It's just that after the first thirty minutes of the show everything goes missing. And while Gerry is talking or playing a record it's very likely that somewhere in the background a producer or assistant is frantically sifting through the mountains of paper, tapes and empty coffee cups for the information on the next item for the programme.

'Guess what, Paul, there's only forty-five seconds left on this CD,' Gerry smiles as the producer races out of the studio to find the tape of the 'Three Old Men'. The only place he hasn't looked is on his desk in the office upstairs. The only one of the Ryan team to sit down on the job is Ryan himself when he sits in the studio.

The tape is found with just fifteen seconds to go. As Gerry goes back on air Paul loads the tape into the machine and sets the player on 'pause'. Then all Gerry has to do is release the button and the show slips into the next item.

The studio itself measures 12 feet by 12 so there's just about enough room to swing a cat. But Gerry hasn't pulled that stunt yet. In front of the presenter is a desk with slide controls on each side. The set to his left

And Gerry loves to talk.

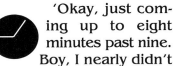
'Okay, just coming up to eight minutes past nine. Boy, I nearly didn't make it there. I put on the nearest available pair of jeans this morning and of course all my money was in the other trousers. So when I got to the toll bridge I dipped my hand into my pocket and found absolutely nothing...'

Paul slips into the studio with the article about the woman eating the snake, as well as carrying in a small heater from upstairs. He bangs the heater off the edge of the door which makes a loud noise.

'Oh, thanks for the noise, Paul,' says Gerry as he recounts his story about the toll bridge.

'No problem,' he replies from the back of the studio.

'Yes, studio-smashing sounds supplied by Paul Russell there. What's this? My God! Snake Found In Woman's Body! That's what it says here.' Then Gerry launches into the story of the snake with maximum fervour. Things are looking good.

Upstairs Brenda and Barbara have decided to do a story together about blindness. Brenda is going to blindfold herself, travel into town by bus and go shopping with just the aid of a cane. Barbara will go with her but she will in no way try to help her colleague. The aim of the story is to find out just how difficult it is for a blind person to manage on the city streets and to see how helpful people are around her.

Back in the studio Ruth is on line three with a disgusting story about a snake after hearing Gerry's newspaper report.

'Ugh! That's really disgusting, Ruth. And you say the snake got into this person as a simple egg in drinking water. That's really horrible.'

'Yes, Gerry, I thought you'd like it!'

'I did, I did! Thanks for that, Ruth. Bye bye.'

The lines are hopping

The phone lines are hopping red with stories from listeners who have their own terrible tales to tell of snakes and insects. There seems no end to them. Each caller's telephone number is taken in case there's a breakdown on the phone line so that they can be phoned back immediately. By 9.30 the snake calls are still slithering along with one amazing story after another. A man phones in to tell Gerry the

Studio cont......
controls the volume levels of the studio microphones as well as the levels on the three telephone lines that are available to him at any time. To his right are the controls for the two disc players, two CD players and for the tape machines that broadcast the advertisements and sketches such as the 'Three Old Men'. Lying all around him is a messy display of takeaway food and coffee, the day's newspapers, running orders and details on guests who are due in to the show that morning.

Outside in the control room are the two telephones which take in all the calls for the show. Once a caller agrees to go on the air they are put on hold. A message is written out for Gerry with the caller's name and the number of the line.

'Who have we got on line three... good morning, Kathy.' The caller always gets to hear what's going on in the show down the telephone. Then he will push up the control for line three. It sounds just like talking to someone at the end of a phone. There is nothing different about it.

It's only natural that a studio guest will feel a little nervous before going on air. But soon after the red light has gone on and they're talking live, Gerry makes them feel comfortable as quickly as he can. And before they know it, the interview is over and the guest is shocked to find they were talking for over thirty minutes.

But some guests don't just sit there. There was the woman who gave Gerry a back massage. Another day he was hypnotised. Then he was kidnapped. Once he was shaved in the studio. However, on that occasion the guest was very nervous and Gerry had cuts from one side of his face to the other.

On the day of Brenda and Barbara's race to Athens Gerry invited the owners of a Greek restaurant to come in to the studio to display the delights of traditional Greek cooking. Not only did everyone savour the pleasures of Greek food, they also took a fondness to traditional Greek wine. By the time the reporters had finally passed the finishing line, the atmosphere in the Dublin studio was certainly tinged with the aromas of a Greek taverna at three in the morning. The ancient happy habit of smashing plates as a sign of joy and happiness would no doubt have taken place, except that the plates in question were made of paper.

It took a full weekend for the smell of wine to leave the studio.

story of the man asleep in his bed in India. His foot dangled out of the side of the bed and during the night he woke up to find his leg halfway down the neck of a giant snake.

'Ugh! Double ugh! Oh my God, I think I'm gonna be sick. I better play some music!'

Back in the office Joan has spotted another story in the paper. This time it's about dolphins and how some women feel a sexual thrill from swimming with these creatures in the sea. It sounds almost as bizarre as the man's leg in the snake's mouth. And bizarre is a word that's way up there in the Ryan vocabulary. Joan telephones the journalist who wrote the story in the paper. There may not be time to do the story on that morning's show but the reporter is quite willing to wait. Joan goes to the studio down in the basement and tells the team they have an extra story if they need one.

When the show runs out of time to do a call with a listener that call is transferred to the following day's running order. And while all the mayhem tears along in the studio between 9 and 12, anyone left in the office has a chance to prepare for tomorrow's show.

'I have a letter,' says Gerry. The snakes recoil. The BAs take a breather. The producer makes the coffee.

'I am writing to you about a problem with my neighbour. Every morning when I rise, from my window **'Close your bloody window'** I can see a certain man scrubbing intensely the afforestation in his armpits. He then proceeds to wash the rest of his body stark naked in front of a curtainless bathroom window. This puts me off my breakfast.'

The letter writer is looking for suggestions as to how to tell the neighbour to do something about his extroverted washing habits. And, sure enough, the letter writer gets what's coming. The phones go on red alert again.

'Leave some shower curtains outside his front door.'

'Look the other way.'

'Write to him saying you have photographs of his naked body which you will forward to the newspapers if he doesn't stop showing off.'

'Close your own bloody window.'

It's almost 10 a.m. Gerry takes an ad break and next is the 10 o'clock news. Breaks like this act as a natural divider between topics, so as soon as Gerry is back on the air again it will be time for a new story or call. Barbara phones in from upstairs on a number 10 bus. She's with Brenda who is 'blind' for the morning. Along with them is a reporter and photographer from a newspaper who wish to follow the story as a news article for the next day's paper. Barbara has a

portable phone which enables her to do a call live on *The Ryan Show*.

'Good morning, Barbara Jordan,' Gerry introduces the reporter on the other side of the news. 'What's this I hear about Brenda being blindfolded this morning. What's this all about?'

Barbara goes on to describe Brenda's slow but steady walk from the radio building across a busy motorway to the bus stop and how the bus driver got

Brenda Donohue, being assisted during her blind walk around Dublin.

8

Socks

The Ryan Show has always thought of itself as a fashion-conscious trendy. No doubt about it. Just look at Ryan.

So it was no surprise that one day somebody would phone in to talk about jeans. But this caller was annoyed, very annoyed. He had been bounced from a nightclub because he was wearing denims. It's not a new topic but it's one that keeps cropping up all the time. He felt it was a class problem. A person wearing jeans outside a nightclub was regarded as someone who couldn't afford to wear anything better. So why should they be allowed into an expensive nightspot.

This prompted the usual selection of stories from listeners who had also come up against the dreaded dress code in clubs. After a couple of these calls it looked like time to move on to the next topic. But then the final call on the matter took us all by surprise.

'I couldn't get into a club last night because I was wearing white socks.'

'What!' Gerry gasped. 'White socks.'

'Yeah. The guy at the door looked me up and down,' said the caller. 'And he just shook his head and said No.'

'So what did you do?'

'I asked him why. I had on a suit and I wasn't pissed or anything. But he just said, "White socks". And that was that.'

Gerry reckoned it was one of the most unusual stories about dress code he had ever heard. He asked had anyone else come across this attitude to white socks before. He didn't think he'd get any calls. Boy, was he wrong!

out of his seat to help her on board. They would be in the city in a few minutes and Gerry would get back to Brenda's challenge later in the programme. Once again the phones start to ring, this time with stories of frustration from blind people who find it very hard to get around the city.

'But you've got to get out there and try,' says one caller, 'because if you don't you'll spend the rest of your life at home having to depend on other people to ease your life.'

The caller has his own lifestory to tell, about how he lost his sight from a car crash and how he spent years learning how to walk without any vision except for a blur. His story is very moving, and soon afterwards the calls pour in with messages of hope and encouragement for him.

Then it's time for Captain X. Every few months this strange, anonymous listener sends in a letter and a tape. Gerry uses that word 'bizarre' again. This time the tape is a collage of Gerry's voice. Captain X has skilfully mixed parts of Gerry's chatting on the radio so that it says something completely different from what he had originally said.

Who he is nobody knows. Why he does what he does is yet another great mystery.

'Thank you Captain X. And give us a call some time. We'd love to know who you really are. I bet you it's Dave Fanning in disguise,' says Gerry. 'Now I'm going to play a long record for you. And it's not because I think it's a brilliant piece of music. It's just . . . well . . . I'm dying for a poo and the toilet's way down the other end of the corridor so I'll need a little bit of extra time to get there. Back in five minutes!'

Oh oh! Back in the control room a call comes through that nobody wants to hear. It's from the guest who's supposed to be in studio with Gerry. And he should have been there twenty minutes ago. But he's not. His plane touched down only ten minutes ago and he's not going to be in the radio centre for another forty-five minutes. Oh oh!

The guest, a preacher from the US who firmly believes that everybody has a real guardian angel only existing in another dimension, is on a lecture tour of Europe. He has just

Socks cont........

The lights on the phones went for melt down. The great white socks controversy had begun. It seemed everyone in the country had something to say about white socks.

'I'm glad that guy wasn't allowed in. I wouldn't be caught dead with someone wearing white socks,' said another caller. The story was beginning to have the right effect.

The following day a young man phoned the show to tell Gerry what wearing white socks had done for him.

'I went for an interview for a job about a month ago. And everything was going fine. They were asking me loads of questions and I thought I was giving them some good answers.'

'Uh huh.'

'Then one of them says to me: I see you're wearing a pair of white socks. I don't think that would go down very well in here. So I just says: Well, I won't wear white socks any more. But I didn't get the job.'

'So you think wearing white socks did you out of a job?'

'Yes.'

The story went on for the next three weeks with new calls coming into the show almost every day.

'So you say you interview persons.'

'Yes. I interview persons. We tend to hire a lot of young men. And we get an awful lot of applications. What we have is a major problem with the time it takes to interview everybody. So a directive was sent down from management as to how to cut down on this time. And the message was : NO WHITE SOCKS.'

Socks cont........

'This is beyond belief,' said Gerry.

'I've talked to two other guys in other companies and they tend to follow similar guidelines.'

A student in sociology added fuel to the fire by saying that, in his studies, people who wear white socks tend to come from a lower socio-economic background.

'That's baloney,' Gerry replied, clearly at the end of his patience. He had endured weeks of the same sort of stuff and it was too much even for him.

Finally one day Gerry's patience ran out.

'Aaaaagggggghhhhhhhhhhhhh. I cannot believe it. This country is crackers! Completely and utterly potts. We'd a doorman on yesterday who said that he knew for a fact that people who wore white socks and jeans were violent and frequently lost the head. This country is full of eejits, full of absolutely and utterly mindbendingly unbelievably thick people. Please, God, come down and take them away.'

Eventually, the matter of the white socks was settled with some sound advice. They're small, they fit in a pocket and if you want to get ahead get a spare pair of ordinary socks. Just in case.

written a book on the topic and contacted the show some weeks before to arrange a date for a guest spot on the show. But now that spot looks like being missed. And in the meantime the show has to quickly think of an alternative. Poo time is almost over and the long song is coming to an end.

'What about Terence,' Siobhain enquires. 'He rang earlier to talk to Gerry. Will I phone him back?'

'Helloooo?'

'Okay' says Paul, who is still talking to the guest on the other phone.

'Who's on line two,' says Gerry, back on the airwaves once again.

'Helloooo?' Terence chips in.

'Ah, Terence, what do you want?'

'Well, Gerry, I've got something to tell you, but in private like. I can't tell you over the air because . . . well . . . it's a secret, sort of . . .'

'Ah, come on, Terence, tell us. What's the secret. Sure no one's listening. They've all gone away. We're alone now,' says Gerry, trying to entice the ex-hairdresser to spill the beans.

'Ah, no. You're only joking. I know the listenership is dere, Gerry. I get the vibes.'

'Oh, you get the vibes, do you, Terence? Is that comin' from your stomach? Are you gonna get sick? You should have those vibes looked at.'

Outside, Paul is looking at the original running order: the plan which had been set out for the day's show. The plan is not working out. But then again, it never does. At 10.45, just over halfway through the programme, things have to be re-jigged pretty quick. Items from the last hour of the show have got to be used now in order to make way for the late arrival of the preacher.

It's noisy. The phones are ringing, the BAs are taking one call after another. And over all this can be heard the voices of Gerry and Terence arguing with each other on air.

'Well, if you won't tell me your secret I'm going to cut you off,' says Gerry.

'You wouldn't dare,' says Terence.

'Bye.'

'But...'

'You wouldn't dare'

'Okay, let's take some music. It's Ryan on the radio from now till midday. If you want to talk about anything in the entire world...and beyond ... then dial us now on 2830222.'

Paul looks at the running order once more.

'Okay, remember the woman who had the poem to read yesterday about smelly socks. Let's give her a call.'

'But Paul, there's a call on three from a woman who's looking for help.'

The woman turns out to be a housewife whose husband has quite literally walked out the door just a few minutes ago. The team decide to go with her call. In less than five minutes the whole studio is silent, listening to this woman describe to Gerry the events leading up to her husband's leaving her. Her voice is trembling, her emotions running over. The show slows right down to take on her story and everyone is listening.

You can tell when something so real comes into people's homes and offices around the country, for the phone lines go silent. No one wants to miss the moment.

'Gerry, what can I do? He's all I had, Gerry. I know...I know I was bad to him. But he's gone and I can't go on.' She begins to cry.

The mood has shifted now. The tone is intimate, as if there is nobody else in the world listening. She pleads for him to return if he is listening.

'I know there's nothing we can do ourselves to ease the

The mood has shifted now

situation,' Gerry says quietly to her. 'But stay on the line and Nita or Siobhain will give you the names and addresses of a few places that might be able to help. And all I can say is, God bless you. I hope it works out for you.'

'Thanks, Gerry.'

The news at 11 follows, during which a steady line of calls comes in, sympathising with the woman and offering suggestions. One counselling group offers to go out to her right away to help. These and other names are passed on to her. Gradually the tempo begins to pick up again. The first call after the news comes from a woman who can hardly hold in her anger against the man for walking out. It's a reaction that is shared by many.

It's time to go back to 'Blind Brenda' in the city, who is accompanied by Barbara on the mobile phone. They have been walking through the crowds of city shoppers for under an hour and Brenda is finding it a terrifying experience. Her eyes are covered with cotton and on top of them lie a pair of swimmer's goggles. She is petrified, but she must learn fast and Barbara reports back to Gerry that very slowly she is gaining some confidence. Gerry suggests that they should go into a shop and see how much help she receives from the shop assistants. All this takes place on air. Back in the studio Siobhain leaves a fresh cup of tea beside Gerry. Paul is setting up another funny tape to be played later in the last hour. There's only forty minutes to go. And still no sign of the preacher from America.

Never underestimate the public response. Someone phones in and suggests that Brenda should try that journey all over again, only this time in a wheelchair. Nita keeps the name of the caller to give to Brenda. Perhaps she can link up the caller when she takes on the challenge in a few weeks' time.

It's 11.20 and time for Gerry to introduce the 'Three Old Men in a Pub' sketch. Every few days the listener is transported to the snug where Peter, Syl and Ned are having a few short ones. 'And we ask ourselves the question we always ask: what on earth are they talking about?' Nobody knows. But the endless mutterings and thoughts and memories of these three old gentlemen are a big attraction for the listeners.

13

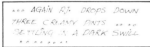

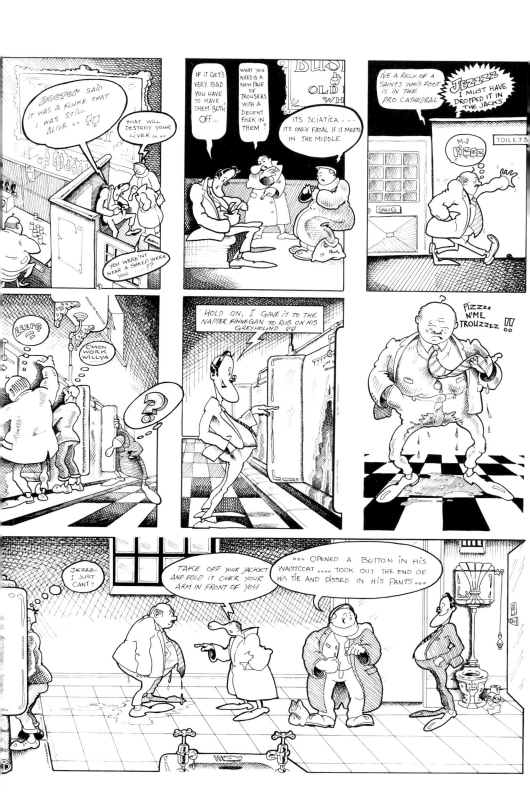

'What will we do next?' Gerry asks, while the tape of the Three Old Men is playing.

'What about the poem about the smelly socks?' asks Nita.

'Yeah. Okay. I wish this preacher would get here. We're running out of time,' says Paul, looking at the clock in the studio. The smelly socks woman is contacted. But she's gone out to the shops and won't be back for another ten minutes. The song is coming to an end and there's no

Brenda Donohue (right) being 'assisted' by Barbara Jordan during Brenda's blind 'walkabout'.

topic to come back to. There are plenty of calls going back to topics already discussed and it looks as if they might have to return to those.

But then, help is never far away. Upstairs in the office Joan has found a story in one of the papers that offers some advice on improving your sex life. Gerry quickly glances through the information and bounces back on the air.

'Hey, listen to this. Here's a few new suggestions on how to have the crack in the sack. Now, are you paying attention. Never mind your candle-lit dinners or your bunches of flowers. It says here you can do the business better if you live on a regular diet of raw vegetables. Ha! Can you imagine. "Darling what's wrong? Why is it so soft? Sorry dear, I forgot to buy the carrots on the way home." Can you believe it.'

Meanwhile out in the control room the tension eases when the preacher and his publicity agent arrive in the door. And the smelly socks woman is back and raring to go:

'This is the story of a terrible odour,

Smelly socks

Of a man with a pong that no one can cure.
His feet are so smelly he's a walking disgrace,
He's got a bag full of socks that I just cannot face.'

The puffing preacher is brought quietly into the studio while Gerry listens to the poem. He is seated next to the guest microphone and handed a pair of headphones. Gerry winks at him as the woman winds up her poem.

'That's very good. Did you write that yourself?'

'I did,' she replies proudly, as a baby begins to cry in the background.

'Oh, what's going on behind you. Is that a baby?'

'Yes it is,' she replies.

'Is it yours, then?' he enquires like a curious school kid.

'Yes, it is,' she answers proudly.

'Oh, so you've had sex then,' he loudly remarks. She pauses for a moment.

'Ye . . . yes I have.'

Gerry's guardian angel

'Oh good. Thank you. Bye bye.'

Twenty minutes to go.

Gerry plays another piece of music and when he returns he introduces the preacher from America. Once again the mood of the show eases down a little as the two men begin their conversation. It doesn't take long before the spiritualist is pointing out Gerry's guardian angel who, he swears, is standing right next to him, in the studio.

But there's nobody there. He explains how no one except a spiritualist like himself can see the angels because they live in a different dimension and are invisible to ordinary people. The preacher insists that if we talk to our guardian angels we will be able to control our lives a lot more. It's a suggestion that's hard to swallow but Gerry gives him all the time he needs to make his points.

Just before 11.55 Barbara phones in one more time for a final word with Gerry about Brenda's challenge. The assistant in the shop has turned out to be very helpful. A small piece of paper with the words: 'Barbara on one' is left before Gerry in the studio.

'Okay, last call this morning from Barbara, who's following Brenda on her blind walk around the city. How are we doing, Barbara?'

As Barbara describes Brenda's ordeal, Siobhain and Nita are taking the last few calls of the morning, mostly from listeners enquiring about the preacher and where they might find his book. Next door the studio lights are on and the next show is ready to go.

'Phew! Good one'

And another morning's broadcast has come to an end.

'Thanks to Barbara and Brenda. And that's about it, then, for today. From me and them until then, that's 9 a.m. on 2FM . . . good morning.'

'Phew! Good one,' he says quietly to himself as the team slumps down in the studio for a well-earned breather. The papers, scripts and tapes are collected into the programme box as well as all the records that have been played.

'Wow!' says Gerry. 'What about that preacher, huh? That was close. If he had arrived any later we would have been too close to the end of the show to do the interview. That would have been a waste.'

Show's over. Time to clean up the mess, left to right: Gerry, Nita Byrne, Siobhain Hough, Paul Russell, Joan Torsney.

18

'Yeah, but what about that housewife,' says Paul. 'She sounded pretty upset.'

'I talked to her for a few minutes after she was on to you, Gerry,' Siobhain adds. 'I asked her to keep in touch with us if your man came back and I passed on a few names of groups that can help her.'

'Brenda's still on the phone,' Nita laughs. 'She wonders if she can stay in town for the rest of the day and go shopping on the show's budget.' The rest of the crew join in on the laugher.

'Typical. Tell her to get her right royal rump back in to the office. There's loads of work to be done,' says Paul.

It's one of the most-asked questions of *The Gerry Ryan Show*: 'Do you all go home when the show is over?' If only it were true! The phones ring constantly in *The Gerry Ryan Show* office all day long. Listeners phone in looking for information about items on the show. They could be about today's broadcast, but more likely they're about a show a couple of weeks ago. All the files are there and it takes some time before many queries are answered.

Agents representing many different businesses, from authors to doctors, even preachers, are always phoning, looking for a spot on the show. Journalists call, offering or looking to interview Gerry, usually relating to a story on the show. People phone in out of the blue with suggestions for the show. It's not always possible to do them but if there's a spark of an idea then perhaps it will work. They are always looking for Brenda and Barbara to visit them and do a live report for them, be it a complaint about a hole in the road, or a demonstration against the closure of a library.

All the newspapers, both Irish and English, are read from cover to cover to see if there are any suitable stories, from interviewing the owner of a dolphin farm to a member of the public who was wrongfully imprisoned. All these people have to be contacted during the afternoon.

Then there's the post. Bags of it. They look for autographs, they look for advice, they look for addresses of help agencies from pet bereavement counselling to groups for the elderly. And amongst the many requests are letters from listeners offering their opinions and stories on topics suitable for the programme. The show doesn't like to rely on letters. They prefer if the letter writers talk about it themselves. So, if there's a telephone number on the letter, they will usually try to contact them and ask them to come on the show.

The afternoon is a hot, bubbling melting pot of all these avenues of work. The central pin, however, is the programme meeting. That's the 'go' siren for the second half of the *Ryan Show* day.

After lunch, at 2 p.m., the team

Conference time meets at the 'round table' in the 2FM offices. It's conference time . . . and sparks usually fly.

'What have we got?' asks Joan, who's chairing the meeting. Tomorrow is her turn to produce the show, so she calls the shots.

The leftover calls from the day's programme are slotted on to the running order. And any guests who had been previously lined up for the next day are also allotted a certain time. Tomorrow it's the turn of a private detective who's talking about her profession. One day she phoned in to the show, out of the blue, responding to a topic, and after a chat on the phone she agreed to come into the studio.

Team meeting 2 p.m., left to right: Gerry, Paul, Siobhain, Joan, Nita, Barbara, Brenda.

'The *Naomh Brendan* were on to us. They'd like to do a call tomorrow if that's okay,' says Gerry, referring to the Irish submarine whose hilarious adventures have been entertaining Ryan's audience for the last three years. The call is added to the list.

'I know,' says Gerry. 'Let's do the show from the sub. Yeah, and we can do a few dives during the three hours, maybe chase a few whales or something.' His face lights up at the thought of it.

'Yeah, but where are we going to find some whales for tomorrow's show?', Barbara enquires, and quite sensibly too.

'Yeah,' Gerry muses. 'Maybe we'll leave it for a few days. Are there any whales around Ireland, anyhow?'

The meeting usually runs for forty-five minutes with each individual member of the team pitching in their own suggestion for the next day's show.

'We've got a computer bible to give away as a prize in a competition. How will we do it?' The table

Pretend you're God

is silent for a moment. Then . . . 'Pretend you're God and everyone has to answer questions from the Bible.'

'Get them to read a passage from the Bible as fast as they can under a minute.'

'Ask them to play their favourite saint and what would they do with the world.'

Joan settles for Gerry playing God. Sounds like a reasonable request for twenty minutes of the show.

Barbara has been asked by a listener to swap jobs. She is a housewife who wants Barbara to do *her* job for a morning while she does a report for Gerry. Barbara hopes it can be done for the following morning but it all depends on how the housewife's family react to the idea. She will find out later on. But for now it's back to the phones and the papers and the post.

At 3.30 Gerry and Paul go into the studio once more. There is a call to be recorded from New York. In a tiny park in Manhattan thousands of New Yorkers have claimed to have seen the statue of the Virgin Mary move.

An Irish journalist is there and wishes to do a phone call report for the show. But that would mean her having to do the call halfway through the night as New York is five hours behind Dublin. To make things easier, Gerry records the call in the afternoon. The tape is then ready for broadcast the following morning.

Back in the office Terence is hollering for Gerry.

'Where is he, Siobhain? I've got to talk to him,' he asks.

'Sure weren't you talking to him this morning, Terence. What do you want now?' Siobhain asks.

'But I couldn't tell him my secret. We were on the air. I have to talk to him now.'

'He'll be back in about a quarter of an hour, Terence. I'll get him to phone you.'

The station manager, Bill O'Donovan, marches up to Joan's desk with some pages in his hand.

'I think these will need a reply,' he says, dropping them on her typewriter. She knows what they are: complaints.

Every week the show receives its own share of complaints from listeners and each one has to be answered. They could be about the use of a bad word, the coverage of a sexual or moral topic or the odd opinion from a listener who didn't believe that a guest on the show was the genuine article: a phoney. Whatever the complaint, it is taken seriously.

Gerry returns from the studio.

'Could you give Terence a call, Gerry. He sounds upset,' says Siobhain.

The items on the following day's show are starting to take shape. It looks like things are coming under control. And then Gerry lets out a roar...

Gerry receives a prank death threat.

'YOU'RE WHAT?'

'YOU'RE WHAT?' he shouts down the phone. 'GETTING MARRIED?... TERENCE... CONGRATULATIONS.'

'Hold the front page,' says Paul. Gerry puts the phone down.

'Did you hear that? He's been trying to tell me all day. He's getting hitched. But he doesn't know how. She's said yes. But neither of them have a clue about how to arrange a wedding. So I told him he *has* to tell the listenership about it, and maybe they'll help him. He'll be in the studio tomorrow morning at 9 to do the announcement. So we'll need a few more wedding stories for tomorrow.'

By 6 p.m. the show has taken on a different shape. It's wedding bells stories for the first hour with Terence and calls from listeners offering him advice. Then the show resumes its original look.

The day is almost done. Joan is the last to leave. As she reaches over to switch on the telephone answering machine a call comes through. She lets it ring. Will she answer it or not. She should be gone by now. But she lifts the receiver all the same.

22

'Hello, is that *The Gerry Ryan Show*,' the caller asks.

'That's right. Can I help you,' Joan replies.

'Yes. About that preacher you had on this morning. Could you tell me the name of his book?'

It never ends

Joan sighs. 'Hang on a minute.'

It never ends.

Nita Byrne, broadcasting assistant, researching during the afternoon.

Vampire

If Count Dracula had a telephone number he'd have been on *The Ryan Show* by now, probably as an adviser. Gerry has talked to every ghoulish and grotesque oddity from one side of the world to the other. But the Count's a hard man to catch during the day.

In March 1990 Gerry managed to track down Dr Stephen Kaplan, a researcher into the paranormal and director of the Vampire Research Centre in New York. Because of the time difference of five hours between Dublin and New York, Dr Kaplan had to take a call from Gerry in the middle of the night. But he didn't mind.

'It's my favourite time of day. This is when I get all my research done, ' he told Gerry in a blood-rich Brooklyn accent. He explained to Gerry the different types of blood hunters.

Vampire cont........

'A vampiroid is a person who resembles a vampire. They live the life of a vampire but they're not really vampires. Vampires don't do that type of nonsense. Vampires must drink the blood of a human. That's not a psychological state, it's a physiological need. Over 80 per cent of the vampires we have interviewed used the biting method.

'Vampires are light sensitive but can wear a cosmetic make-up or cream during the day to come out, although they prefer the evening.'

Dr Kaplan went on to explain that he liked to research vampires instead of hunting them. He didn't wish to have them exposed to the gaze of the public and so kept the identities of his vampires a closely guarded secret.

'By and large they're mostly pleasant people, and most of the humans that they get their blood from are willing rather than victims. They drink the blood two or three times a week with other foods.'

So what does the Vampire Research Centre do?

'Vampires come to the centre and we try to help them. By the way, the centre is not a dating agency for vampires. We collect information. This is not a joke. This is a very serious business. In fact I just turned down a TV show about vampires because they were passing off vampiroids as vampires and I didn't want to be associated with that.'

He went on to reveal that there are over 600 vampires throughout the world. He pointed out that they had received confirmation that there were two living in Ireland.

'Some vampires do work in hospitals but they don't take the blood once it's withdrawn because there's an anti-coagulant put into the blood in hospitals. Some nurses will, however, take a sample of your blood and say they're taking it away for analysis when in fact they're drinking it next door.'

Dr Kaplan then explained the contents of his latest invention: the vampire kit. It's a box that contains garlic, onions and a mirror, and its aim, apart from tracking down vampires, is to protect the tracker.

'And you know, we've discovered something. Onions and garlic work against vampires but not if you hang them 'round your neck. You have to swallow the stuff. That's what makes the difference.'

Well, you'll never know these things unless you ask.

History...

Bill O'Donovan popped his head round the door of the office.

'Got a minute?' he asked. Cathal McCabe looked up from under his glasses to see who was asking.

'Yes. Come in,' he replied as he got out of his chair. He walked over to the stereo in the corner and reduced the volume. He had been monitoring the programmes on the station which, at that time in February 1988, was known by its full title as Radio 2FM.

'I might have a plan' Bill was the station's manager. A tough character who wouldn't take any nonsense from either presenter or producer. He was always open to new ideas, so long as those offering them could accept a straight 'no' in reply. But then, occasionally, an idea for a show would catch his attention.

'It's about the new slot for the morning show.' Bill paused, watching his colleague's every movement. 'I might have a plan.'

Cathal McCabe prepared himself. As the head of music and variety on all programmes on RTE radio he took the responsibility for any changes in that department, be it on RTE Radio 1 or 2FM, classical music or pop.

'What about putting Ryan on the radio from 9 to 12,' said Bill. The words popped out as if he were asking to borrow a pen. Cathal smiled. **'I don't appreciate your sense of humour'**

'Bill, I've always known you as a man who can tell a good joke, but really, I don't appreciate your sense of humour.' Both men laughed. The thought of putting that rascal on the nation's airwaves during the morning was somewhat comical, especially if he was going to talk. Gerry talked enough already at night time.

His show at the time ran between 10 and midnight. It was a mixture of music and chat, with Gerry doing most of the chat. Occasionally he would talk to listeners on the phone and ask for their opinions on the latest pop releases. And outside of that most people knew him only for his claim to have killed and eaten a lamb while reporting on a survival course he was taking part in for *The Gay Byrne Show*. When it was revealed that he had never killed the lamb the 'spoof' or 'Lambo' incident made front-page news. It also made Ryan very famous, one way or another. And many top people within RTE believe it did him more good than harm.

Gerry's night-time show was a safe bet, sitting comfortably **'A steady supply of hits'** between the specialised listening of Dave Fanning's rock show and the late-night sounds of Mark Cagney after midnight. Together the three presenters earned a reputation for offering an individual style to night-time radio. One Irish magazine at the time named the three collectively as 'The Right Stuff'.

Daytime radio on the nation's pop station at the time provided a steady supply of hits from the Irish and international charts.

'The Right Stuff', left to right: Mark Cagney, Gerry, Dave Fanning.

There was little room for anything else. In many ways that was the most sensible thing. Radio 1 was just the flick of dial away where you could listen to talk all day long. There was enough waffle on the radio already.

But daytime Radio 2FM was becoming a bit of a headache. And no amount of popular music could soothe the audience figures into climbing the ladder.

'Radio 2 didn't have a high-profile show,' producer Willy O'Reilly reflects. 'It was up against the wall to find one. Management said it was time to take a risk. If they hadn't done that they wouldn't be sitting in their offices today.'

The telephone rang in Cathal's office, interrupting the conversation. It was a call for Bill. As he handed the phone across the desk to his colleague Cathal lifted up a report lying in front of him. He studied its contents once again. The document was a time survey showing what the average person did with their day: what time they got up in the morning, what time they took a break from work. The report concluded that there was not a vast audience of young people listening to the radio in the morning. So perhaps there was room for something more than just music.

He thought back to the meeting of all 2FM staff a few days earlier to discuss new programme ideas. The answer was the same. Something more than music.

Bill put the phone down.

'D'you really think Ryan would work?' Cathal asked.

Something more than music

'Look. If the big bosses don't want him off in the first week, and the public don't want him off in the second week, then I'll fire him myself in the third.'

'Okay,' Cathal smiled once more. 'Let's give it a try.' The time for risks had finally arrived.

The first *Gerry Ryan Show* went out on Monday, 14 March 1988. The running order for that day included Gerry's opinions on St Patrick's Day postcards, a competition offer of a fortnight in Dubai, a report by presenter Andy Ruane on the making of a Hothouse Flowers video for the Eurovision Song Contest and an interview with sports presenter Gabriel Egan. The formula was rigid. But even on the first day Gerry departed from the order and took some calls from curious listeners.

The original crew for the show included producers Maggie Stapleton, Pat Dunne and broadcasting assistant Joan Torsney. To put on a three-hour radio chat show for five days of the week was a huge undertaking. None of them knew what route the show would take or what limits they could take it to. But it was a challenge, something to prove.

'There was a young, spirited team effort there,' says Cathal. 'A group of young people who felt they were looked down upon by the heavyweight programmes over on Radio 1. There was an element of: we'll show them. They took the challenge upon themselves. That has been sustained to the present day.'

Early days 1988. Left to right: Willy O' Reilly (Producer), Gerry, Pat Dunne (Producer), Joan Torsney, Maggie Stapleton (Producer) .

In front of that team, in front of the microphone, with three prime-time hours of radio space to fill, Gerry also had much to prove. No matter how many topics could be discussed or reported on in one show he realised early on that he would still have to 'wing it' for a lot of the time, to bring together whatever skill and experience he had developed over the years of broadcasting and bear it all down upon that microphone and his audience.

As the weeks inched across the year's calendar Gerry's real character came out from behind the voice, into the open. And listeners responded to this openness.

Instant radio 'Gerry was the full exponent of instant radio,' Pat Dunne explains. 'He would unleash a string of thoughts and descriptions on what was happening. He showed he had a gift for talking at length with no notes or scripts. It was a very unusual attribute.

'In the fallow periods, when we didn't really know the show's identity, Gerry used this period to expose the bad things, the things that can go wrong, the hiccups in the studio, something breaking down. He created dramas out of anything that happened. It was, quite simply, mistake radio and it went totally against the seamless radio of other chat shows, the type that try never to make mistakes.'

28

Topics in those early months also hinted of things to come. They ranged in everything from married women returning to work, to breast cancer. Then in April Gerry reported on a drastic world shortage of shepherds, while in May he gave away fifty pairs of women's knickers. From the start the serious was interwoven with the ridiculous.

'For the first couple of weeks the phone reaction was very poor,' says Maggie Stapleton, a producer with Gerry at the start. 'So we put out an apology. It was an apology for the show. We used Ian Dempsey's voice to apologise for Gerry being on the radio. So everyone then was asking, well, what did he do to have to apologise in the first place. Then we put an apology out for the next day's show. I think then people copped on that it was just a gag. But it caught their attention.'

It also caught the public's disgust.

'The listening figures didn't increase immediately,' says **So somebody was listening** Bill. 'But after about three months they started to climb. That never eased the pressure of complaints, however. The public continued to complain about Gerry and his style of broadcasting. They felt their attitudes were being assaulted. But if people weren't paying attention nobody would have complained at all. So somebody was listening.'

The numbers continued growing slowly as the top presenters on Radio 1 took their three months' annual leave from the start of June. It left the airwaves wide open for another show to make its mark.

We really went for it 'Because the big shows were off for a summer season we had no problem getting guests and good stories. There wasn't all that much on Radio 1 that summer so there was no clash. We were out on our own. We really went for it,' Maggie remembered.

While producing other programmes on the 2FM schedule Willy O'Reilly also contributed items to the show. From the very start he saw what was happening to make the show successful.

'Back then we didn't know just how much Gerry could carry. But it became very clear that Gerry's personality could carry a large part of the show. That point was actually spotted by Gerry's colleague, Dave Fanning. You can have the best producers in the world but if you don't have the voice to carry the personality and ideas then you're lost.'

One morning Gerry broadcast the show from a shop front as part of a promotional deal. It was a miserable, wet morning with just a few people quickly rushing past Gerry's window to get indoors. But instead of gently pleading for an audience to turn up he went on air saying, 'Incredible. Just incredible. I've never seen so many people crammed in to one place before. And I don't know what the weather's like in your area but here the sun is splitting the skies. I can see marching bands going by and everyone has come out to have fun. It's just brilliant.'

Within twenty minutes his view was dotted with people who came from all around to see the carnival. All they found was an empty car park with some DJ sitting in front of a microphone. No crowds, no bands. No sunshine. And only one person recognised who was presenting the programme.

In June and July of 1988 the show delved into such topics as banning skate boards, small fish being strangled by used condoms in Dublin Bay, dead animals on the side of the road, problem neighbours and transvestites. If management had been edgy about taking risks on the airwaves there was plenty of reason to be very edgy now.

'We once got into trouble for using the word knickers, can you believe it?' Maggie

Concorde...

On the last Friday in September 1988 Gerry found an envelope sitting in front of him down in the studio. There was a message inside.

'Dear Gerry, the past few months have seen you work with little reward, entertaining the Irish public. Today for a change we want to entertain you. We have set a task for you. Your mission, should you choose to accept it, is to follow a set of clues prepared for you. Once you accept the initial offer you must follow the path to its conclusion.'

Talk about putting a red rag to a bull.

The first clue led Gerry out of the building and into a limousine waiting outside. All this time he kept a link with his studio through a mobile phone. DJ Colm Hayes sat at the controls and played music while Gerry was whisked to his next clue, somewhere in the city.

For the next two hours he and his listeners were taken on a mystery tour around Dublin, never knowing the final destination until almost the very end. Callers to the show offered their suggestions to each new clue. And every little bit of help only added to building the tension – where was this all going to wind up? Nobody knew, least of all Gerry.

Finally he found himself close to his own home in Clontarf. Time was running out. There were just twenty minutes to go on the show when he received the last clue. It led him to the back garden of a private house. What he saw in front of him made his eyes pop out of his sockets.

Concorde cont.......

'It's a helicopter,' he roared down the phone, 'sitting in the middle of the back garden.' He leapt in to the cockpit to be told he was being taken out to the airport to the enquiries desk of Air France.

But he wasn't the only one heading in that direction. The back roads to Dublin airport began filling up immediately with listeners who had been tuned into the show and decided to follow the posse, for real.

Touching down at the heliport Gerry noticed a new addition to the fleet of planes. An Air France Concorde was standing proudly next to the departure zone. The terminal building started filling up with listeners following the story and who were themselves astonished to see the slick supersonic bird parked under their noses. They had not read of its arrival in any newspaper. So the journey was worth taking after all.

Gerry made his way quickly to the Air France desk. All the time he kept talking by phone that hooked his voice on to the airwaves. It's not often that you hear Gerry talking by phone to his own show.

The end of the whole magical mystery tour arrived when a representative with Air France handed a white envelope over to Gerry at the counter. It was a ticket for two to Paris. Their mode of transport was that very special aircraft waiting on the runway outside.

'I couldn't believe it,' Gerry remembered. 'I thought our day's work was finished at 12. But then I was told I was spending the weekend in Paris. I wasn't even packed. But did I care? I don't know what I said on the air at that moment, but I think it was very rude.'

explains. 'Cathal McCabe used to reprimand us. We were always being monitored. There were memos sent all over the place and tantrums raged whenever a curse word was used. But the public didn't seem to mind.'

The team had good friends in Cathal and Bill. Everyone involved in the early stages of the show became aware that they were receiving only a fraction of the total complaints. People would phone the show on the Ryan line to complain. That was a daily occurrence, and the broadcasting assistants would deal with those irate calls. Siobhain Hough recalls getting calls to the studio from listeners saying: 'Get your man off the air, he's crap.'

'Once we had a wild woman on talking about her sex life,' recalls Joan Torsney, a former broadcasting assistant with the show and now one of Gerry's producers. 'The call was very risqué and explicit. I mean, she didn't hold back any physical description. But later on a workmate told me he had been out walking that morning and these people were running out of their houses telling their neighbours to switch on the radio and listen to what was going on on Gerry's show.

'Sometimes people phoned the show to say they were fed up listening to so much sex. One woman asked Gerry on the air could he not talk

Concorde cont.......

The full effect of Gerry's treasure hunt was a huge turn-out from listeners to see the world's only commercial supersonic aircraft as it stood on view, waiting for its special guest to quickly phone his wife and ask her to pack a case of clothes for two.

about anything else. He asked her for a few suggestions and she told him he could do some stories on flowers and dogs. So the next day we devoted the whole show to flowers and dogs.'

But complaints of a stronger nature, including those coming from within RTE, would be dealt with by the station's management. Both Cathal and Bill stood by the show as it stretched out its arms over the airwaves.

Gerry broadcasting during UCD's World Debating Challenge in Belfield Dublin, 1988.

'The first two years of the show were extremely difficult for us. We placed ourselves between Gerry and his detractors,' says Bill. 'There was a constant battle going on behind the scenes to keep him on. The trick was for us to stop the flak from reaching Gerry and to allow him the freedom to do his own unique thing on the radio. We were severely criticised for doing it. But Gerry's show set a new precedent.'

'Once the phones **Gerry's show set a new precedent** started to ring, that's when Gerry started to shine,' says Maggie. 'He was very eager. We were all very eager.'

The list of contributors began to grow as interest in the programme developed. Radio 2 News had plenty of stories to report on that were not strictly newsworthy, but they were perfect for Ryan. Reporters for the show included Orla Guerin, now a

Early Days. Gerry with Andy Ruane, 2FM DJ and a former contributor to the Ryan Show in 1988.

correspondent for television news, Dave Fanning and television **Free and easy** presenters Pat O'Mahony and Andy Ruane. Ruth Buchanan contributed to the show.

'I remember doing a couple of reports. The format and style appeared very free and easy. They discussed every possible idea. There was nothing barred from the reports. We could do anything, so long as it was short. To me it was very clear what was happening on that show in 1988. And it was also very clear that the show was going to develop. There was no doubt about it.'

One morning during the summer Joan Torsney arrived into the studio with Gerry. It was a Monday. Joan searched for the running order that was supposed to have been prepared the previous Friday. But no one had done it. There was no plan for that day's show.

'What!' Gerry said as Joan explained she hadn't been in on

Making a drama out of nothing

the Friday. Someone had been skipping off. But that wasn't the point. What were they going to do for the show that morning!

Joan frantically ran her fingers through the newspapers looking for items that Gerry could mention. And, using his old rule for making a drama out of nothing, Gerry went on air at the start of the show to announce that they hadn't a thing prepared for the programme and did anyone have suggestions. He was asking his audience for help, for real.

'And it worked,' says Joan. 'I found a few

Mistake radio

stories in the newspapers that Gerry read out from time to time during the morning and he would get reaction to the stories. Then people phoned in to suggest items for discussion. We made a three-hour show out of absolutely nothing.'

Across the road from RTE, the students in UCD Belfield took to the airwaves themselves for one day every year. Radio Belfield was an experiment in broadcasting usually held during the college's entertainments week at the end of term. Willy O'Reilly went to Belfield each year to help out.

'We'd rehearse everything before going on air. The shows would run for a couple of hours each. We had three studios,

Brenda Donohue (left) and Barbara Jordan (far right) with two singers from the public during their outside broadcast of songs from 'The Sound of Music'.

Turkey...

Sometimes a festive season can bring out the best in a person. Take Christmas. Now there's a peaceful time of year if ever there was one. Unless, of course, you were listening to Gerry on Christmas Eve in 1988.

'Wanna kill a turkey? Live? By phone? Then dial us now on 830222 and play Shoot The Turkey.'

The animal world mightn't like it but the humans certainly did. The rules were simple, if you knew how to play along with Gerry. A contestant would go on air and choose his or her weapon. Throughout the whole ordeal listeners could hear the sound of hundreds of turkeys clucking around Gerry's feet.

'You can choose between gun, bow and arrow or grenade. What'll it be?'

'Gun please.'

'Okay now, all you have to do is direct me towards a turkey. Give me any order you want. Tell me to go up, down, left or right . . . or whatever. Then when you think I've got him in my sights, tell me to fire. Okay?'

'Okay.'

'Are you ready?'

'Yeah.'

'Okay . . . Go!'

'Right, Gerry, up a little . . .'

'You want me to go right, then up a little?'

'No, just up a little.'

'Okay, tell me when to stop.' The orders carried on until the caller was convinced they had a turkey in their sights.

'Ahhhhhhhhhh, sorry, you missed him. You got the producer, though. Do you want a producer for Christmas?'

including the Roadcaster which we used to call "Mother". The programmes were usually very successful.'

Brenda and Barbara

One of the students who did reports for Radio Belfield in 1988 was Barbara Jordan.

'Barbara had a friend called Brenda Donohue. Sometime later when we were looking for new people to do reports I remembered Barbara. She started doing a few reports. And after a couple of weeks Barbara brought Brenda on to the show as well.'

Compared to the professional reporting of the journalists working in RTE, the early taped reports by Barbara and Brenda were awful. Everyone agreed. And Willy dished out severe bursts of criticism that could be heard from one end of the building to the other.

'We had terrible rows. Some of their reports were just too bad to put out on air. I edited them to try and make them sound even half acceptable. But underneath it all we knew they were different. That was their advantage.'

By October both Brenda and Barbara had picked up some of the skills of interviewing. They weren't winning awards but their fresh style and energy complemented the fun aspect of the show.

'Then one day we found what we were looking for in the two of them,' Willy recalls. 'It was a feature about the Dublin buses. We put Barbara on one bus with a mobile phone and Brenda on another. They were to try and find out how fast the buses were getting into town and ask passengers for their views on the service.' The item ran throughout the show and provoked thousands of phone calls. It ended with Barbara being thrown off her bus, live on the show.

'It worked. It was the first coherent phone topic. At the time the newspapers said it was a brand new form of broadcasting. The mobile phone became their forte overnight. They suddenly became, in a way, Gerry's representatives on earth.'

Nothing stood in the way of the show as the big names returned to Radio 1 in the autumn. More and more people were talking about what Gerry Ryan did on the radio yesterday and what he could possibly do next. It could be selling gallstones on air, brain

Turkey contd........

'No thanks, Gerry.'

The calls continued for the next hour. Some callers bagged their turkey. Others just chipped off bits of the studio.

But there was one little problem. There were no turkeys. This was just a furtive slice of imagination for the final show before Christmas. So how was Gerry going to get out of this one?

'Okay, which weapon do you want?'

'Grenade.'

'Ah, at last. Someone who isn't afraid of a bit of noise. Are you ready?'

The caller began to give his aiming orders, until finally he was ready.

'FIRE.'

There was a loud explosion in the studio. The turkeys reared up and started fading away.

'OH, NO! You've missed the bloody turkeys and blown a hole in the wall instead. They're all escaping ... the turkeys are escaping ... help!' Gerry roared as he ran out of the studio, chasing them.

The turkey shoot wasn't the only crazy competition on *The Ryan Show*. There was the 'Guess the cheese challenge' where listeners had to smell the cheese down the telephone line and then name it. Then there was 'Blow Job' where contestants played blow football by telephone.

Usually there is a prize at the end of the ordeal for the winner. Companies offering prizes have to agree at the start that the competition may not be exactly to their specifications or liking. And in a number of cases the firms in question have backed down and refused to take part. But, on air, the challenges always turn out to be crazed rituals of overacting by both Gerry and the contestants.

surgery in the studio, killing rats with an electric stun gun, discussing the fluff in belly buttons or contacting Elvis beyond the grave using a medium in a live seance.

In fact, Elvis has been very good to Gerry.

A fantasy world that the listener could join

'One day we were short of an item,' Willy recalls. 'Gerry read a bit out of a newspaper about Elvis being spotted alive. So Gerry said he'd heard a rumour Elvis was in Ireland. He asked listeners had anyone seen him. There were phone calls from all over the country, from Elvis himself, Elvis's daughter, and an Elvis Presley was reported to be working for the Corporation.'

'That was the day that we realised that if we presented listeners with a scenario then they would do the rest. It was where Gerry could conjure up a fantasy world that the listener could join.'

Producer Pat Dunne knew the show was catching peo-

Looking into the madness

ple's imaginations when he saw assistants answering phone queries long after the show was over and replying to letters looking for more than just a record request.

'He was capable of looking into the madness. He had great insight into what people were capable of doing. Gerry alerted people to the possibility of having great gas on the radio.'

The biggest-ever reaction to a topic on the show occurred when a caller phoned in to say that flying saucers had been spotted in the skies over Kildare. That one single call prompted almost three hours of sightings, apparitions and strange phenomena from all around the country.

Callers also phoned in regularly looking to work on the show. They felt they could contribute to the programme with their own selection of anecdotes and opinions. Some names have popped up regularly ever since, like 'Mrs Vile' and 'Pat'. But one name stands tall above all others. And that name is Terence.

'Terence came as a counterweight to Gerry's character. He filled out the

'Tell it to Terence'

heart of the programme,' says Pat Dunne. He was the first to talk to Terence on the phone and immediately the voice at the other end made him smile.

Terence was a camp hairdresser from Cork who loved his mother and had an opinion for everything. Unfortunately his opinions got him into trouble with his employer, and shortly after joining the show as a regular he found himself out of a job. The nation felt sorry for this poor soft-hearted man who summed up the woes of the world with his primary belief that 'We're all God's children'.

Soon after Terence was fired Gerry offered him a regular spot on the show on Monday mornings

Dragonae...

One day a man phoned the show to say he had an insect that he would like identified. Gerry asked him to drop it in to the office. The man agreed.

That afternoon Gerry was handed a jam jar with an enormous dragonfly inside. The insect looked very unusual. Its colour was yellow, its legs stretched the length of the jar. Its giant wings looked compressed as they wrapped themselves around the body of the insect.

No one had noticed that the lid of the jar lacked any holes punched in it to allow in some air. But by the time the intrepid scientists had discovered the reason why the dragonfly was not moving it was too late. The insect was dead. It came as quite a shock to the team. Nobody had ever died on the show before.

There and then *The Gerry Ryan Show* decided it was their responsibility to bury the creature. One of the team felt so guilty about not saving the poor creature that she spent the entire night designing a special coffin. The insect itself lay in state in the drawer of the producer's desk with a 'Do not disturb' sign attached to it. The following morning the *Show* presented: 'The Burial of Dragonae'.

Slow-marching music accompanied the grim ceremony as it got underway just after the start of the programme. In a sombre tone Gerry explained to listeners what had happened the previous day. There were many calls of sympathy to the programme. The coffin was made of wood, its lining made of purple silk. Its

38

called 'Tell it to Terence', where the man with an answer for everything would avoid answering anything if he could help it,

even down to the hundreds of letters that began pouring in for this, the country's only agony uncle. The questions would range on anything from contraception to how to hide toenails under the bed.

On New Year's Day 1989 Gerry decided to send his season's greetings to a few people around the world. They included the Queen, Margaret Thatcher and President Reagan. He phoned them live on air. Sadly, however, none of them were home. And their assistants weren't very helpful.

'What d'ya mean you want to talk to the President,' said an official at the White House. 'That'd be like phoning the Queen and asking to speak to her,' he laughed.

'Yeah, we did that. She didn't want to speak to us either.'

Surveys on audience figures for *The Ryan Show* in the early months of 1989 showed a huge surge of listeners. Gerry was winning new ears by the busload every week. At the same time he was receiving a record number of complaints on anything from him belching on air – a habit he still likes to bring up from time to time – to his coverage of topics like strippers, both male and female.

The letters included one from a listener who said she was going to ask her entire neighbourhood to refuse to pay their television licences. There were also threats of violence. One man phoned to say he was coming into the radio building that morning to 'give Gerry a good hiding' for the terrible things he was saying on the show.

But nothing succeeded in calming the storm. Gerry continued to grow in confidence. So, too, did his team. By this stage *The Ryan Show* crew was made up of two reporters, Brenda

Dragonae contd........

shape was the shape of the cross, to allow for Dragonae's wing span.

Colm Hayes, a former DJ with 2FM, assumed the role of high priest who led the procession from the studio out into the corridor, past the staff toilets and into the courtyard of the radio building. All this time Gerry continued giving the slow-paced commentary, describing a scene of great sadness and pointing out the many dignitaries who had turned up to pay their respects.

After thirty agonising minutes of airtime spent wallowing in pity for an insect that had been dumped in the office in a jam jar and died there a few hours later, Dragonae was finally laid to rest in a hole under a row of rose bushes. It was a hard act to follow.

39

and Barbara; two BAs, Siobhain and Joan; and two producers, Willy and Pat; not bad for running fifteen hours of prime-time controversy every week of the year.

'When we were delving into these no-go areas on radio we were wide-eyed and breathless during the shows,' says Joan. 'Nobody had ever gone this far, so it was really quite nerve-wracking. After each show it was very hard to unwind. So you just worked harder. Sometimes a work day could be fourteen hours long.'

'There was an "x" factor about Gerry's show,' Pat adds. 'A new generation had arisen. They had a different outlook to talk radio and to Radio 1. Gerry himself was different. It was quite special that Gerry could talk about such topics as sex and not sound alarmed or on the defensive. His generation accepted it. He had an ease about it. It was a weird mixture but somehow people accepted it. Up until then there had been boundaries but this was completely new. It was fun but it was serious too.'

The serious always has a place on the show. Somewhere in the middle of the madness as the show tears

Nude...

In the ice-cold regions of February 1990 the last thing anybody wanted to do was take their clothes off for a dare. But that's just what happened in the last hour of *The Ryan Show* one Friday morning.

Two days before the revealing moment, Brenda Donohue had interviewed an antiques dealer with a very curious hobby. He was a naturist and liked to help organise indoor nude parties for his nature-loving friends. Brenda's report provoked a big discussion about what it would take for anyone to strip off in front of a crowd of people, especially in Ireland where continental conduct and freedom to express your body are not admired.

But Gerry decided to take it one step further. He reckoned it would make 'an interesting experiment' to present part of the show stark naked.

Well, at least it wasn't television.

So as not to feel left out in the cold he managed to persuade the rest of the team to do likewise. And at just after 11 a.m. on a cold winter's morning the tiny group of professional broadcasting personnel, who had risked life and limb in the past to bring the best out on radio, assembled in the studio to bring out a little bit more.

Three years before Gerry's all-live nude show, the four members of U2 had stripped down to the nitty gritties on Dave Fanning's *Rock Show* during an interview. But they're just crazy guys. This was a serious experiment. There were tests to be done, reactions to be monitored and heaters to be installed.

Gerry wanted to find out how to fry an egg in the nude without getting burnt or

Nude contd........

how to dance naked at a disco without all the dangly bits getting in the way. All fascinating questions for the would-be naturist.

One listener phoned in to say she was getting in the mood by getting in the nude. She wanted to know if Gerry had a pimply bum. It took the authoritative voice of Gareth O'Callaghan in the next studio to verify that Gerry's botty appeared soft as a baby's.

Another caller wanted to know what her husband might think if he came home to find her cooking his dinner completely starkers.

'If I were him I'd forget the starters and go for the main course.'

Concluding the experiment, everyone on the team had their own opinion on the whole nude show. As for looking at a naked male producer and a male presenter, Siobhain had to admit: 'You found yourself looking ... you know ... at the ... at their ... yokes.'

The landmark bare broadcast was rounded off with the all-live nude rendition of *We'll meet again.*

along like a slapstick comedian, a topic or a caller can be dropped into the middle of the pot like a special ingredient, pulling listeners up with a jolt.

'Gerry allows the people time to talk,' says Pat. 'He nudges people into that area, to talk about things that perhaps they never talked about before with even their closest friends.'

The mood in the studio always changes when someone is talking painfully about their personal life. It could be a death in the family, a story of violence or a caller contemplating suicide. But very quickly all other activity on the show stops. There is suddenly a sense of tiptoeing through a very private and personal part of somebody's life. Joan recalls a listener who phoned the show one day out of the blue. She was pregnant and her parents knew about it. They were forcing her to have an abortion, which she did not want to do.

'She was very upset. She was crying for most of the call. I'll never forget it, though. It was one of the most intense moments I've ever lived through and yet it was on the radio, for everyone to hear.'

It's just a phone call, but somewhere down the line a caller is baring their soul. And half a million people, with carefully hidden souls, are listening in.

'Sometimes they cry,' says Maggie. 'And he never treats them badly or too quickly. He takes them very slowly through what they are talking about and shows that he cares. That's where

The growing pains are over

Gerry in boxer shorts.

Gerry really shines. He can care as well as being an entertainer. Nobody else comes near him for that.'

A caller who is obviously in need of help after telling their story is always offered help, if not by other listeners sympathetic to their plight then by the staff of the show. The Red Box is *The Ryan Show* file with names and numbers of agencies and individuals who can help a caller. It is an essential ingredient in the back-up to the programme.

'Gerry's just an ordinary guy,' Cathal McCabe explains. 'He's not an institution. Not like Gay. His success depends on the absorption of his production. The teamwork has been, and is, vital. The show just grew that way. It wasn't planned every inch of the way. It just took a different route. And its consequences are a cementing of 2FM's identity.'

People have time for Ryan now. The growing pains are over. And the listener is always invited to play along.

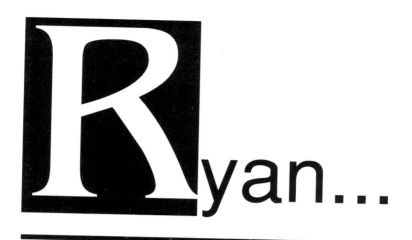

Ryan...

It's hard to look back over the years without instantly thinking of the madness, the lunacy, that has gone into making three hours of radio every day of the year. It's hard to try and remember every little thing and every call and crazy competition.

Bizarre encounters There's just so much that has happened since the day we started broadcasting in March 1988. So many interviews, so many bizarre encounters and events. If you asked me to think of one moment that stands out above all others I would have to reply, 'Only one?'. It doesn't all slot in to the memory banks easily. But there are a few moments I remember. Ones that shaped the way things are for me today.

I can think back to the morning of the very first show. The weather was awful and I had a terrible sore throat. What a start for a talk-show presenter. I had no idea what was going to happen. But I knew I wasn't nervous. I've never been nervous of the radio. Useless maybe, but never nervous.

That whole period happened so quickly. One minute I was hosting a night-time music show, playing the hits and mouthing off once in a while, the next I was in the station manager's office being made an offer I couldn't refuse, if you know what I mean. I really loved the night-time show. I had good company, sandwiched between Dave Fanning's *Rock Show* and Mark Cagney's *Night Train* programme after midnight. We were a trio. We were like a rock and roll band. We even toured together when we worked as weekend DJs, earning some extra cash in the clubs. No one could touch us.

Audiences for night-time shows are so different from the day. After dark, life for most people can get a little quieter around the house, so there's less to disturb you. That's when it's just you and the radio. And that is the time when a presenter is at his or her best – when you know they're listening. It doesn't matter about audience figures and all that baloney. What matters is that they're listening.

Then one day I was called into the oval office. My boss, Bill O'Donovan, had a bizarre plan. He wanted to take me and Mark off the night-time slots. I was to go on in the morning. Mark was to go on at 5 p.m., better known as the drive-time shift, when people are coming home from work.

A little weak at the knees

I didn't want to move. To be taken out of the private world we had created at night was pretty scary. I didn't understand daytime pop radio. It was just one longplaying record. I love music and I've got a lot of favourite bands, like Genesis. But I didn't know all that much about the current music scene, and

I guess we had taken the programme to its natural limit. I preferred to listen to talk shows on Radio 1 and BBC Radio 4. And as for doing three hours each day, well, I knew I could talk all right, but for the whole morning!

So basically I didn't like the deal. But bosses have a terrible habit of insisting. And Bill had his mind made up. I felt a little weak at the knees when I thought of going on air at the same time

The King on his Throne.

44

as Gay on Radio 1. And not only that, but to go on even longer than Gay: his was just a two-hour show.

But we looked closely at his programme all the same, to see how it worked and why. First of all, it was easy to listen to, and anchored solidly by a regular selection of letters from listeners. Gay himself was the primary factor though – a master of personality and opinions.

I guess I had a lot to prove I loved to talk on the air and I had already given it a go. Once a week on the night show I put a couple of listeners on air by phone to review the new singles releases. But it was just an excuse to talk to people, about anything. I'd get the music review over with fairly quickly and then go on to ask some more questions, like if the song had any personal significance for them. You know, sneaking in by the back door, if you like.

I got a kick out of it. But the authorities didn't. I was told to stop the prolonged questioning. I thought it was without any doubt the best bit of the programme, but one guy inside RTE told me to my face that I was rubbish. Looking back, I suppose that was like a love bite compared to some **I was rubbish** of the comments I was about to get.

I guess I had a lot to prove. From the start the show was a bit like a creature from *Star Trek* groping around in space, looking for something to latch on to. But the creature was very determined to get through the three hours and I remembered what I'd learned from listening to Gay Byrne: personality. I had to get that across.

So I thought I'd better start talking to them. There were a lot of things in my head that I wanted to let loose, lots of different things, mostly about people, I suppose. We all think we know a little about people. What I knew was that people like to hear about themselves, about their own lives, right down to the colour of their neighbour's butter dish.

The production team was tiny. They also had to work on Mark's new drive-time slot. That meant I was going to have to do some items of my own. Nobody planned it this way. That's just the route it took, the only one available. There were a lot of rows in the early days. But we kept the fighting behind closed doors. Sometimes it even happened in the studio, during a song or an ad break. We'd roar at each other if something had gone wrong. But it was the adrenalin inside. Nothing personal.

Then there were the people who thought that I was crap. Just plain garbage, bringing down the tone of the station and RTE as a whole. They were extra-ordinarily rude. But they were listening all the same. That was the first time I realised we had an audience!'

A locust sandwich

I remember the day we had an item on about a new range of bizarre exotic foods. I discussed the nutritional value of sinking your gob into a locust sandwich or getting your fork around some good wholesome larvae tagliatelle. It was disgusting. But I loved it. I love that sort of stuff, the horrible gooey stories like the one from a caller whose son was bitten by an insect on Killiney beach, and when they cut open his arm they found hundreds of little dead insects that had been born inside his arm. It was horrible but oh, can you imagine it! People love to hate ugly topics like that. It's part of the enjoyment. It's mind-boggling the number of people who say some of the stuff I do is horrible and disgusting and then the next minute they're telling me a story that's even more disgusting.

What I really enjoy is having crack on the radio. I get as much kick out of the stories as the listeners

Fortune Teller..

Towards the end of 1989 a regular reporter on the programme suggested getting a series of predictions for the next year from a fortune teller. Tom Higgins, who specialised in topics of a more bizarre nature, took a tape recorder along to meet professional fortune teller Deirdre Montague.

The tape was then edited down to reveal some of the more interesting suggestions for events in the future. And on the first day of the show in 1990 Tom's recording of Deirdre Montague's visions of what lay ahead was broadcast. That was the last Gerry expected to hear of it.

The following November Tom Higgins listened back to the tape and nearly fell off his chair. He phoned Gerry.

'Remember the fortune teller you had on the show in January. Well, I've just listened back to her predictions and . . . well, I think maybe they're worth broadcasting again. Almost everything she predicted has come true.'

A few days later Gerry broadcast the report once again. Her facts of the future, recorded in late 1989, proved deadly accurate.

'There will be a big lotto win in April . . . possibly two million.'

'Ireland will make it to the last eight in the World Cup Finals in Italy next June.'

'Margaret Thatcher will resign.'

She also predicted that Soviet Premier Gorbachev would face a constant assault on his leadership from the opposition but that he would survive. And some time in the future President Bush would be

Fortune Teller cont........

assassinated. So she didn't get everything right. But for most of the report her peek into the future was indeed deadly accurate.

Since then Deirdre Montague has become the *Gerry Ryan Show* resident fortune teller.

Everybody's got imagination

do. But it's not all as it seems, you see. That's the fun part. The essence of radio. You can't see it. You have to use your imagination and everybody's got imagination. It's the one thing in life that doesn't need a training course. That's what I like. I knew the show was working when friends started to ask me: 'About that guy with his ear sewn on to his stomach – was that true or not?'

After a couple of months of that everything started to change. Listeners started to get a handle on it. I sensed the reaction was coming from a new, young, middle Ireland. They were game ball for anything. People used to phone in looking for a request and I'd cut them off. Then they started to cop on to that as well – don't ask for requests, unless you're very brave or just crazy.

I'm not saying it's easy to talk to people live on the air, but I was feeling a bit more comfortable with the contact, a bit more confident. People have often asked me is there a delay device built in to the system where a call can be monitored before it goes out on air. The answer is no, and if there was it would cut the lifeline of the show. It's all about being absolutely live.

Then one day I remember a caller who, without realising it, completely changed the rules of talk-show radio. And it left me shaken to the core, believe me.

Her name was Majella. She was from Finglas. She phoned in

An ordinary Dub

one morning in response to a guy who'd just been on talking about women. She wasn't angry, she was just giving her own opinion. But every second word she used was 'fuck'. If she earned a pound for every time she said it she could have bought me dinner. They just flooded out on to the airwaves like tiny little gremlins saying, 'fuck, fuck, fuck'. My whole body was beginning to sweat like I'd just inherited malaria. I could see the bosses upstairs blowing a fuse for every 'fuck' she let loose.

But she was genuine. Pure and simple. The words she was using were just part of her natural vocabulary. An ordinary Dub. In fact she didn't even know she was cursing. And I knew this. So I tucked my hands under my bum on the chair and refused to cut her off. It was the most difficult experience I'd ever gone through, like not scratching an itch.

So she finished her piece and went on her way. I can't remember a word she said, except the words in question. We wrapped up the show and then we sat there, in the studio, for what seemed like an awful long time. I was expecting a squadron of executives to swoop down any moment and take me away. Eventually we slipped up the stairs, hoping that no one had heard the broadcast, which is a bit like praying for snow in July. Bill O'Donovan, the man who put me there in the mornings, walked up to me and calmly said: 'That's the first time I've heard anything like that. If this was the army you'd be court martialled and kicked out on your arse.'

That was the last I heard of it, except that it got a fair few mentions at the meeting of the RTE Authority. But I felt we'd come through something very important. Everything changed after that. The tone of the calls changed. People felt more relaxed talking on air. It was like they could say what was really going on inside their heads and their hearts. They didn't feel like they were going on display.

Naughty on the radio

I think that call was the key to a room full of human secrets that no one had ever dared enter before. I know now that because of these secrets and some of the other stuff on the show the heads of 2FM had to take the brunt of complaints from both outside and inside RTE. They kept that away from me. I only discovered that recently.

Sure, I've been naughty on the radio. What's the point in going on air and doing the same thing as everybody else. We needed something different, a little wilder. And when I thought about it, all I could see was John Cleese and Monty Python doing the silly walk sketch on TV. I wanted to do the silly walk on radio.

To go one step further

I thought about this a lot at the time. How was I going to go one step further than anyone else. I could talk, yes. But there had to be more to it.

A caller phoned in once to ask me a question, I think it was about underpants or something equally important to the structure of the universe. I don't remember the actual advice I gave, but I remember how I said it. I squeezed my eyelids tight and spoke in a high-pitched voice, totally different from my own.

'Ahhhhh, my lit-al glasshopper, you have a question for Fu Man Chu.'

Suddenly I was a different character. I was an evil Chinese hoodlum who had just taken over the controls of the studio. And I wouldn't let go. I answered every call like that, for about an hour, unleashing these high-pitched wails and trying to talk like I had a ferret stuck up my bum, and a Chinese ferret at that. But that was the start of it. Like everything in the show, we had stumbled by pure fluke on something new. After that, there was no stopping my newfound skill at becoming somebody else, including the Ugandan dictator, Idi Amin, who would threaten every caller with execution.

'Come on, lady, dis is de last chance you've got or Idi's gonna slice your neck off.' And people would play along. They'd start saying 'Yes, Mr Amin. No, Mr Amin.' Then I would start talking to another character called Dr Caligari, created and performed by my

The search for the 'new sound of 2FM' promotion March 1989.

49

old producer and friend, Pat Dunne. 'Cali' was like a cross between Frankenstein and Ghandi. So now the team was beginning to get in on the act, which was tremendous. The listeners liked the crack. We liked the crack. We just didn't know what it meant.

Frank Maguire

Of all the voices, though, the one which had been building up inside me the most was that of a character called Frank Maguire. A complete bastard. A loud, drunken Irishman who loved the gargle and hated everybody who wasn't a native. The kind of man that I hate more than any other. He came into existence, rather fittingly, on St Patrick's Day 1989. I'll never forget him. That deep, drunken Irish voice. You could almost smell the whiskey and the fags as he roared abuse at anyone and anything that didn't have a *fada* in it. Pure vermin. That oldtime Irishness really makes my blood boil. And that morning I must admit, I let it loose. Callers pleaded with me to take that feckin eejit off the air. But for me he was the personification of an old Ireland that should have been buried years ago. Instead, we buried him that day.

It's hard to know sometimes how the programme is shaping up, how things are sounding. It doesn't matter how much you analyse it, it always seems different in the studio when there's people whizzing around you. But I never know what it actually sounds like on the radio. So after each show I'll call the one

Gerry with his wife, Morah, after he received a Jacob's Award for the show, October 1990.

50

person who I know can give it to me straight. That's Morah, my wife. She never holds back an opinion. If it's good she'll say it. If it's bad I'll get the gorey details.

Sometimes I think she should present her own show. She once phoned up the programme to take part in a quiz. I mean, she knew I was doing the show. But she phoned the studio and faked an accent to get on the air. I remember it was a quiz to find a Southern Belle, an American damsel and the prize was a bottle of champagne, I think.

I got this message to say that 'Liz' was on line two, so I put her on the air. I never realised it was Morah. She put on this thick American accent and she was so good at playing the damsel that she won the champagne. My own wife. It was Ian Dempsey who sussed it. He phoned the studio to tip us off. But it was too late. I had declared her the winner, totally unaware of the trick.

No. She didn't get the bubbly. We tracked down the runner-up and gave it to her. I had to buy Morah a bottle myself. Otherwise she would have brained me.

Gerry, 4 years old, as Darby O' Gill at the Stage Guild Ball, March 1961.

I used to play with a tape recorder when I was a kid. I'd get a few friends around and we'd try and record some funny sketches on tape, paying homage to the routines of Monty Python. I had no idea then that fifteen years later I'd be recording sketches for a living.

The object of our comedy sketches is simple: just cause chaos, be it demented, deranged, hilarious or, hopefully, all three. The most deranged of them all has to be the 'Three Old Men in a Pub'. It's one of the longest-running items on the show – just three old guys trying to make sense out of the world without ever really finding the answer. To this day I still get calls from barmen all over the country telling me that they have those exact same characters coming into their pubs every night of the week. The beauty of it, however, is none of it is scripted. There are no rehearsals because there's nothing to rehearse. Once a week three men meet in a studio, the tape is switched on and they start to talk.

Live surgery

Two people who helped turn the early sketches into more than just a laugh were DJ Colm Hayes and Radio 1 producer John McKenna. Colm's a very talented broadcaster. My one regret is that we couldn't keep him on the programme. John McKenna added to the fabric of the show in a way that most people will never know. Just believe it. That's the magic of his contribution. We've had explosions in the studio, pagan rituals, live surgery and interviews with groups like 'The British Blood Cult', a society that celebrated blood by extracting it from its victims using the most bizarre methods. We got a lot of stick for that. Of course, these would always be woven in with the rest of the show's contents. But, you never can tell.

Stevens...

'Please do not give this telephone number to anyone', the voice pleaded. 'It is most important.'

The producer agreed and took the special London telephone number from the girl. He had to wait five more minutes before dialling. Time was pushing on towards the end of the show. The interview was planned for the final hour between 11 and 12. Perhaps the chat would only last a couple of minutes. Nobody knew what was going to happen because no one had actually talked to the guest. It was yet another risk.

'Hello?'

'Hello, can I speak to Mr Yusuf Islam, please?' Paul asked.

'This is Yusuf.'

'This is Paul Russell from 2FM. You were expecting a call from us this morning to go on air to Gerry Ryan. Is this time okay?'

There was a pause at the other end.

'Eh ... well ... could it not wait a little while?'

A little while. Why? Did he have to go out? Was there a sermon he had to give? Was he expected in class?

'It's just that ... I've just poached some eggs for my breakfast,' said the cockneyed voice. It had taken a number of days to set up this interview with a man who once used to call himself Cat Stevens. The former pop superstar had turned his back on the material world ten years ago for the rigid rules of the Islamic religion. *The Ryan Show* had to abide by these same rules in order to get him to go on the show.

And now this ordinary voice at the other end of the telephone wanted to wait until he'd finished eating his breakfast.

'But I suppose I can heat them up afterwards. This isn't going to take long, is it?'

It had taken long enough to set up the interview in the first place. He wouldn't talk to any woman on the show. It had to be a man. Then before going on he had to see the questions that Gerry was going to ask him. And he had to approve of the songs to be played during the interview, all of them belonging to his former self: Cat Stevens.

More than twenty years before, this same man was riding the crest of a pop wave that would carry him well into the Seventies with songs like *Matthew and Son*, *Lady D'Arbanville*, *Peace Train* and *Morning Has Broken*. Then just before the Eighties rolled in, he took on his Muslim name of Yusuf Islam and walked away from it all.

He now spends his life in prayer and teaching the lessons of his religion. And, as a Muslim, he believed that the author Salman Rushdie should be sentenced to death for writing *The Satanic Verses*. When this former champion of peace and love throughout the world publicly went along with an execution order from the Ayatollah Khomeni the world was indeed outraged.

And while the questions in the interview were aimed at seeing how Yusuf spends his life, underneath it all, Gerry and his listeners wanted to know if Cat Stevens was still in there, somewhere. The interview ran for the full, final hour of the show, revealing a compelling mixture of beliefs and opinions.

He explained how in 1976 he was given a copy of the Islamic Koran. By that

One thing you could tell, though, was that the complaints were hitting the roof. Producers of the show have to grow an extra layer of skin to take the calls and letters of disgust and revulsion from listeners. I believe some of those letters are as disgusting as the topics they refer to.

Somewhere in the middle of all this, when we were still trying to find our feet, or at least where we'd put them, the media caught on to our act, and stories about us began appearing in the newspapers. We picked up titles like 'tabloid radio' and 'zoo radio'. I'm rather fond of zoo radio myself.

Zoo radio

But whatever way they tried to box us in we were still doing something very new. We were allowing spontaneity to take over. The tapes, sketches and interviews in each show are always scrappable in favour of the moment, whatever that moment might be: a call, a comment or an incident. Whatever is happening, if its part of the public arena then we'll make room for it. We still work towards that moment. It's in our veins.

It's hard to define what we do. I'd have to go back to the philosophy of *Star Trek* – to boldly go where no other show has ever gone before. To reflect instantaneously what people think and feel and at the same time to entertain people in a way that they'll never forget. To continue to go places is a major challenge, a challenge to our integrity. And that's very evident if the show gets boring. Sometimes that happens. Not for long, though. But if it were to continue we'd have to give it up.

My one fear is that I will become mechanical in my approach to the show. And that goes for the team. We can become more professional. We have to. But if we were to become like a routine – even a very successful routine – that would actually strike at the heart of the idea of the show. If that happened the show would be dead.

If I had to design a motto, then, for what we do it would be: 'Crack and Concern'.

We always make way for a serious call. It's very tense when listeners talk to me and reveal part of themselves through some event or problem in their lives. When I know this is

Stevens cont.......

stage in his life he was fed up with the pop world and needed something more. He does not respond to his former name. He does not have a record player. It all seemed very certain.

Yet Gerry persisted.

'But Yusuf,' he asked. 'When you're having dinner and maybe you've had one or two more than you're supposed to and one of the guests says to you: come on Yusuf, play us one of the old songs. Would you not give in. Do you not remember them?'

'I remember them,' he replied. 'But as to playing them again,' he paused. 'I don't know,' he giggled. He went on to explain how he had turned up in Wembley Stadium for Live Aid in July 1985. The world had come to save lives and Yusuf had agreed to play. It would have been one of the high points of the day.

'But there wasn't the time. They could not find a place for me on their running order. I was very disappointed.'

As the interview progressed a warmer, kinder voice crept out from behind the brutal image. And as the conversation went on the calls flooded in; calls from Cat Stevens' fans as well as from those wishing to ask Yusuf for his opinion on the Salman Rushdie death sentence.

Gerry strayed from the music as well as the questions. After playing *Peace Train* he asked Yusuf: 'Well what do you think of that song now?'

'Not bad. Not bad at all.' There was a special warmth creeping into his voice, a friendly human manner that, as the conversation went on, became more obvious. He talked about the time he spent in the studio recording his songs and how one 'cut' or version was better than another. For a while he sounded like another man altogether. The change in tone and enthusiasm for the interview was very noticeable, sending shockwaves through the studio.

Finally Gerry got around to what by now most callers were asking for.

'If you were in the same room as Salman Rushdie, would you do the deed. Would you kill him yourself?'

For the only moment he was truly stuck for words. Gerry never got an answer. He didn't pursue the matter. He didn't need to. He had found a man within another.

'Sorry about the poached eggs,' Paul said to him once the interview was over. He showed no signs of anger at having been put on the spot about Rushdie. Yusuf won a new band of admirers that day, many of whom had come closer to understanding the man behind the mask of another set of beliefs, a faith that is as distanced to the beliefs of the West as it is distanced in miles.

happening – and I usually don't until maybe seconds before they go on air – I've got to clear my mind of all the things that have been happening on the show. Nothing else matters. I'll psych myself down and honestly ask myself am I capable of answering or responding to this situation. The response has got to be honest. People can spot bullshit a mile away.

People imagine that I go upstairs and brood about a call for the rest of the day. But I don't. I can't do that. The moment the call is ended so is my contact with that problem, otherwise there would be no to-morrow. I would be a total wreck and I can only presume that counsellors and psychologists deal with it the same way.

Alan Only once has something on the show stayed with me long after the interview. In early 1990 we broadcast a story about two young men in their twenties who were both suffering from Cystic Fibrosis. I spoke to Alan McGovern and Stephen Nesbitt. Alan wore an oxygen machine that made a little hiss right through the interview. Both men looked quite frail. Stephen looked the stronger one. It took Alan about ten minutes to walk from the radio building entrance to the studio, a journey that normally takes a minute. The energy used in that walk alone would have kept another person going for half a day.

They both knew how debilitating this disease is. Alan said if he didn't get a new set of lungs and a heart then he would die. But both were full of spirit and genuine humour and together they showed how to stand their ground against their illness. It was a genuine shock to the system. I had to do a double-take during the interview, to pull myself up in case I'd display any feeling of pity. That was the last thing they needed.

Their story haunted me for a long time. I can't explain why. The show has had many guests with incredible stories to tell, mind-boggling experiences from all parts of the world. But there was something very real and human about what these two friends were going through. One night, almost a year after the interview, Alan popped into my dreams for what seemed like a split second. That was all. A short while later Paul Russell told me that Alan had died.

His father came on the show to tell us what had happened. His message was that everyone should carry an organ donor card. Life is the greatest gift. He produced a series of pages from a note pad. They contained the last thoughts Alan ever tried to communicate with his parents. His agony was scrawled across the pages, almost like a young child trying to write for the first time. Sometimes they rolled off the edge of the page, almost incomplete. But George McGovern explained each indecipherable word to me. They made references to the pain and to ending it all and to his wish to be free of this disease.

His last word was 'Balls'.

Alan's death enhanced the value of life for me. It was a very special experience to meet those two men.

So we were succeeding on many counts. The media began pitting Gerry against Gay. I didn't really have an answer for that one. I didn't see us in direct competition. We weren't looking to take him on. After all, he'd invented talk-show radio in Ireland.

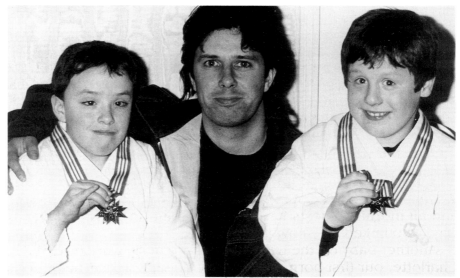

'Star' Achievers, two disabled boys pictured with Gerry in 1988.

But we did do something pretty naughty on him all the same. It was back in 1989. I went to a party on board one of the Irish Navy ships, the *Eithne*. I must say I was on top of the world that night for one very special reason. That was the night Morah told me she was expecting our second child. Some time later on that same night, after getting to know a couple of the crew members I was told, on the sly, that Gaybo was going to be broadcasting his show from the ship very soon. In the midst of my personal euphoria, I kept a note of the date.

Ireland's only submarine On the morning of the broadcast we hooked up a special radio link to our studio so that, when I pushed up one of the controls on my desk, the listeners could hear Gay's show as well as mine. Every couple of minutes I'd say 'I wonder what Gay's up to now' and I'd push up the control and Gay would be talking to some member on the *Eithne*.

The scene was set.

It just so happened that I was interviewing the captain of Ireland's only submarine, the *Naomh Brendan*, that morning. The coughing, spluttering captain of this totally fictitious tin bucket (whose source of fuel was anthracite) informed me that at that moment he was about to initiate training exercises not a million miles away from the *Eithne*. Then disaster struck. The *Naomh Brendan* fired a torpedo, completely by mistake and heading straight for the *Eithne*.

I'll never forget listening to Captain O'Brien's emotional account of the sinking of the Navy patrol ship while at the same time we listened to Gay calmly going on with the show as if nothing was happening.

But something big had happened. Something pretty nasty, now that I look back on it. *The Gay Byrne Show* wasn't too happy with our prank. In fact, there was murder over the sinking afterwards. But eventually we made our peace with the Radio 1 camp, and maybe even a few new friendships were forged.

He joined me one year later for what was to be our most complex broadcast outside the studio, even though we were only fifty yards down the corridor. We decided to hold an outdoor party on the morning of the People In Need Telethon in 1990. We moved everything out into the courtyard of the radio building, and all morning guests kept popping their heads in, including Gay, who linked his show up with ours.

Another baby on the way. Those were really wonderful days. Charlotte, our first-born, was almost three. She had been born at a time when daddy hadn't a clue what he was going to do

DID U KNOW

FACTS

A HISTORY OF THE L.E. NAOMH BRENDAN

BY JOE TAYLOR . . . .

DESIGNED BY J.P. HOLLAND (LISCANNOR CO. CLARE) ... BUILT IN HARLEM + WOFF DERRY.... 1904 A.D.

AT THE LAUNCHING KING EDWARD VII SAID IT WAS A SHAME TO WASTE A GOOD BOTTLE OF CHAMPAGNE ON SUCH AN UGLY LOOKING "YATCH" AND DRANK THE BOTTLE HIMSELF.

SHE SAW ACTIVE SERVICE DURING W.W.II .. ..
THE BRITISH ADMIRALTY DENY ABSOLUTELY THAT SHE WAS RESPONSIBLE FOR SINKING THE LOUSITANIA OFF THE SOUTH COAST OF IRELAND .. " " "

DECOMISSIONED IN 1935 SHE WAS SOLD TO A FALKLAND ISLAND SCRAP DEALER WHO LEASED IT TO GENERAL FRANCO IN 1936 .... SHE WAS RENAMED L'INQUISICION,

BY 1970 L'INQUISICION WAS BRING-ING PLEASURE TO HOLIDAY MAKERS ON THE COSTA DEL SOL, AS THE "JUAN CARLOS SUBMARINE SANDWICH BAR"

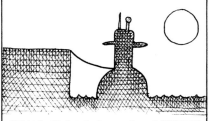

BOUGHT BY A GROUP OF COUNTY COUNCILLORS (ON A HOUSING JUNKET...)
IT WAS DISMANTLED AND THEN RETURNED TO HAULBOWLINE IN CO. CORK. THERE SHE WAS FITTED WITH A NEW ANTHRACITE AND TURF BURNING ENGINE...

PHELIM CONNOLLY 41

with his life. He certainly didn't think he'd be hosting a talk show. But now things seemed that little bit more promising.

Charlotte was looking forward to the new addition. Home life for her is the same as any other child's. Except that she's got two slightly cracked parents to contend with. Somehow she has managed to separate me from the broadcaster. One night we were watching TV together and my face popped up on the screen. It was a recorded interview. But Charlotte looked at the TV screen first, and then at me.

'Look, dad,' she said, 'There's Gerry Ryan.'

With Jean-Anne Crowley and friends during The Ryan Show 'People in Need' Garden Party, May 1990.

Two slightly cracked parents

Somehow I knew Morah would have the baby while I was supposed to be doing the show. There are twenty-one other hours in the day. But she wasn't happy with that. So I had to phone the station and say 'Eh, I won't be coming in today. We're expecting a visitor.'

I'll never forget one of the most bizarre experiences of my life. I was waiting for Morah to give birth. I was sitting there trying to calm my wife as well as three other women in the ante-natal ward. Outside in the corridor a woman was screaming. She hadn't made it to a bed before the baby started to arrive. She was screaming, Morah was upset and I was trying to comfort everybody. Just then a woman stuck her head around the

59

door and asked me for my autograph. In the middle of all this! I just couldn't believe it. I was stunned into taking the paper and signing my name, automatically. And as if that wasn't bizarre enough, she then started to talk to me about a recent item on the show. I actually started talking to her about the programme item while my wife began to moan in labour, the woman outside was still screaming and, God knows, the other women in the ward were probably roaring as well.

Gerry thanks God after signing a new contract with RTE, 1990. Director of Radio Programmes, Kevin Healy, asks why.

Morah gave birth to our first boy a few hours later. The following day I went back on air. The word was out already about where I'd been the day before. But I didn't mind. I was on top of the world. I wanted to talk about babies and birth and post-natal classes and childcare and anything breathing that was under five years of age. But somehow the producers managed to hold me back.

The show never leaves you, though. No matter where I go I'll always meet somebody who wants to offer a suggestion or go over some topic for discussion. I used to respond to it a lot easier in the earlier days. We even

The show never leaves you

organised a couple of dinners for regular callers and guests so as we could talk about the show and its contents and get plastered at the same time. But now I don't go out as much to public places. It's just inviting interruptions from people who want to talk about the programme. It isn't fair, for either me or them. And if I don't want to talk, then I shouldn't be there saying no, go away. I prefer dinner parties and drinks at home with friends. But when I do go out I love the crack.

Once, however, I remember I had to get away. A woman accosted me in a supermarket. She turned me around and started firing these single-word comments at me: filthy, dis-

She hit me with her handbag

graceful, awful. Then she hit me with her handbag.

And like a complete idiot I asked her what her problem was. Well, she exploded. She just went completely off the rails, telling me how awful the show was and backing up her attacks with accurate quotes from the show. That, of course, meant she was listening to the bloody thing every day. So I said to her, 'Well, if you don't like it, why don't you switch over to Gay?'

'He's worse!' she said. I couldn't handle it. I had to run away and hide in the fruit and veg. department. But it was a real eye-opener. There are some people who genuinely hate the pro-gramme. I only hope I don't meet them all together. Certainly not in a supermarket.

Back in 1989 there was a lot of talk about the impending threat of independent radio. We were being prepared for the onslaught of legal competition for the first time in the country's history. Up until then, of course, there had been the pirates – Nova, Sunshine, Big D – of which I was a member for years before joining the brand new Radio 2 in 1979.

We had all been plucked from the pirates. And now it looked like some of us were going to be plucked back. Colm Hayes left for Capital, now Rock 104; Marty Whelan went to Century and Mark Cagney moved to 98FM. I was offered a lot of money to move, and on the face of it the offers looked very tempting. Even

The Ryan Show's first birthday celebrations, left to right: Willy O'Reilly, Barbara Jordan, Gerry, RTE pal John Creedon, DJ Colm Hayes (formerly with 2FM), Pat Dunne, Siobhain Hough, Brenda Donohue at Judge Roy Beans, Dublin, March 1989.

61

members of the production team were approached about the possibility of moving with me.

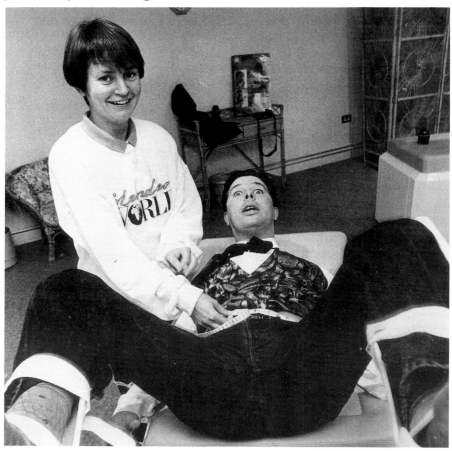

Shaping up at Slender World.

Out there on its own
But some risks are too great. Nobody knew what the future held for independent radio as first Capital, then Century and later 98FM went on the air. I never considered those stations as a threat. I always viewed *The Ryan Show* as 'Radio Ryan', out there on its own. 2FM was without doubt the better place to broadcast from, considering the team that I had behind me and the support I was getting from the station's controllers.

But even so, there were times in the first two years when I was very worried about the future. It was great crack, but would I survive. More importantly, would I be allowed to survive. No one was telling me that they were delighted with the success of the show. Things have a habit of changing very quickly. And for

Brenda Donohue (left) and Barbara Jordan freshen up for the show in Sicily, May 1990.

a long time I stayed at the edge of my seat, waiting to be pushed off. But it wasn't going to be without a fight. I realised the honeymoon was over. We had stretched the limits and made a few eyes pop out. But the more successful the show became the more we knew that research and back-up were going to play an even greater role. That proved itself vital when I went to work in TV.

If there's one bit of back-up that I love to depend on in the show it's when Brenda Donohue and Barbara Jordan are out on the job. Their style of reporting gives a whole new meaning to the word 'professional'. They are true professionals. They'll go to the ends of the earth to report for the show but when they go on air I feel I'm talking to two friends.

Of course, they weren't exactly professional when they started out. In the first few months of the show we had many different people doing stories for us on the air. Then I started hearing about these two women who were fresh out of college and offering ideas to the show.

'Students!' I thought. Oh, no, they'll probably want to do book reviews or something incredibly boring, which is exactly what they did. And they weren't very good at it, either. But, God love them, they persisted. They were just as hungry to prove their worth to us as we were to RTE. And somewhere down the line our ambitious plans met head-on.

It's like something out of the Keystone Cops. Sometimes their style is slapstick. I remember the day the two of them went out looking for communion dresses. Brenda played the mother, brilliantly. She was this prissy woman, looking for a very conservative style of outfit. Barbara played the fed-up kid who had her eye on one dress and nothing else would do. She may be in her mid-twenties but that morning she was the personification of the downtrodden child who whinges all day long and tugs at your jacket to keep moving.

In the Canaries with his wife, Morah, March 1991.

A story that will pin you to your seat

Another day they'll have a story that will stop you in your tracks. I remember when Brenda spent a week living on the dole. She took help from no one. She did it as only she would – for real. Barbara has found some extraordinary stories for the show. But the most astonishing has to be her series of reports from Romania. All her defences were down. She was raw and vulnerable from having seen so much suffering in that country. It took great courage to do those reports.

Everything in my personal life influences me when it comes to the show. There is, in fact, a serious overlap between my private and professional lives and there's diddley I can do about it. I don't come into the office a half hour before the show and make up special thoughts for that morning's programme. Everything I say is the way I am, right down to the hangovers. To tell you the truth, most of Monday morning's programme is usually a hangover. And I

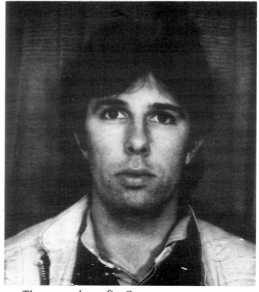

The morning after?

64

Focal...

It's not that *The Gerry Ryan* Show doesn't like politicians. They just don't put them on in the first place. So when the headline: 'Burke pulls 2FM plug' appeared on the front pages in May 1990 nobody on the show phoned Dáil Eireann.

The Minister for Communications, Ray Burke, had announced that 2FM was to be closed down and an educational radio channel was to be put in its place. He also said that three million pounds in licence fees would be diverted into independent broadcasting. RTE reacted angrily to the new plans. *The Gerry Ryan Show* reacted in the only way it knew. They decided to become an educational programme overnight. No point in wasting time!

The following morning, after the news at 9 a.m., listeners were given a taste of things to come.

'Good morning and welcome ... to *Focal* ... or word ... in Irish. My name is Gerald Ryan and today we'll be continuing our Spanish lessons for corporate businessmen. There's a special report from Brenda Donohue on cloud irregularities along the west coast and Barbara Jordan will be in the studio talking about the growing trend in ... POP music.

'And we have a repeat broadcast of a repeat we had on *Focal* yesterday about the many wonders and mysteries of book binding. A very popular choice.

'But first on *Focal* I'll be talking to a man who knows a good story when he hears one. His name is Tomas O'Ceallaigh and I'll be talking to him for the next three to four years about his life on the by-roads of Ireland during the years 1939 to 1978.

know it suits the mood of many listeners, who may not necessarily be suffering brain-disordering pain from the excesses of the weekend but there's a reasonable chance they're feeling a little ragged and slow to burn right at the start of the week. Once I know that the country is behind me on that one I can get on with the show. But there was one day, and it wasn't a Monday, when a hangover got the better of me.

Feeling a little ragged

There had been a 2FM party in the Burlington Hotel the night before. It sort of went on, and on and on. So the next day, a Tuesday, I was feeling pretty ropey and the last thing I wanted to do in the entire world was to have to talk for three hours. But there were lots of items to get through: interviews on the phone, guests in the studio – the works.

Fortunately everyone else on the team had been to the same party. Coffee was on an intravenous drip. The studio was full of farts and bad breath. So maybe that contributed to me puking during the show. That's one disgusting incident that I decided to withhold from public broadcast, until now.

But I vomited my guts up during that show. I have no idea what I was talking about at the time. I know I was talking to someone on the phone. I felt this hot sweat seeping through the top half of my body, like an alien had just invaded my stomach. Oh, oh, I thought. This isn't going to stay down any longer. I thanked the caller very quickly and instead of going to the next topic I said, let's take a piece of music. Like bloody quick. I got up out of the chair, my head started to swerve in front of my eyes like a rollercoaster. And there was still two hours of a show to go. I just made it in time to the toilet where I paid dearly for my sins of pleasure. And I can tell you I didn't feel any better for the rest

Never again of the show. I felt kie-boshed. Never again. I swear, never again. I used to be able to come in with a Grade A wogga wogga hangover but I can't do that any more.

The only other form of pain that exists in the studio is Terence. That man is without doubt the fussiest gobshite it has ever been my misfortune to work with. Unfortunately, he also happens to be the most gifted and definitely

Focal cont........

That's on page 47 of the yellow manual on story telling for beginners. And I can tell you it'll be a great yarn, heh heh.'

Politicians got the message in *Focal*. Hands off.

Later that year another politician faced the full force of public opinion. Brian Lenihan swore blind he didn't phone the President to avert another general election. The taped evidence said he did. And suddenly, what was turning out to be a dull, lifeless presidential election campaign in the autumn of 1990 became a hotbed of intrigue and drama.

Naturally enough, the bed was big enough for Gerry to slip in between the sheets for a bit of foreplay. No politician was asked to come on the show. Instead, the reflections, opinions and thoughts were left to the public to air their views.

And just to add a little spice to the discussion Gerry also asked listeners to make up *The Ryan Show* Top Ten songs for Brian Lenihan. Top of the Pops never sounded better. In reverse order, the final list was:

Stand By Me – John Lennon
Take A Chance On Me – ABBA
You're History – Shakespeare's Sister
When The Going Gets Tough – Billy Ocean
I Won't Back Down – Tom Petty
The Theme from 'Shaft' – Isaac Hayes
Celebrate: This Party's Over – An Emotional Fish
Sorry Seems To Be The Hardest Word – Elton John
I Should Have Known Better – Jim Diamond
Always Look On The Bright Side Of Life – Monty Python. From the movie soundtrack of (of course) 'The Life Of Brian'.

Terence is a star the most hilarious character to have ever phoned the show.

Things happen by accident for a lot of the time on the programme. And Terence was the *numero uno* casualty. He tripped on to the show one morning and from the very start I knew this man was going to be a star. Sounds a cliché, I know, and no one believed me. But it made me feel like a fairy godmother to offer him a regular job as our agony uncle.

For a couple of months he did personal appearances at clubs and concerts. And on one occasion we did a double act. I've never seen anything like it. It was like a scene from the American evacuation of Vietnam. People clung to Terence like he was a god. And all he did was give away plastic copies of his spectacles. I mean, what else could he do!

The best form of therapy But Terence is a star. He'll always be up there, among the big name figures, like Olivier, John Wayne and Goldilocks.

Just like the radio, it's always a relief to turn it off when you've had enough. I do my best to keep the weekends for my family and myself. Otherwise I'd be a complete pile of jelly. It's great to be a slob on a Saturday afternoon. To do absolutely nothing at all. It's the best form of therapy.

At the other end of the scale, however, there is my love of flying. During the second year of the show I was offered a set of lessons in a helicopter. I'll never forget the experience of being handed the controls for the first time as we flew over the Irish countryside.

'Me? You're letting me fly this thing by myself?' I thought the pilot was completely mad. Up until that moment I didn't think I'd have the nerve. But I did it. I can't say it was the prettiest bit of flying. In fact I can't remember the flight at all. I was shitting myself until the pilot took back the controls.

Up in the sky, totally alone The greatest achievement of my entire life had nothing to do with broadcasting whatsoever. It was the day I did my first solo flight, with no pilot to turn to. Being up in the sky, totally alone, viewing the world from those giant cabin windows is without question the most exhilarating experience. And when I finally touched down, my brain was still up there somewhere in the clouds.

I could talk about machines for days. Planes, trains and submarines. If someone rings the show looking for advice about anything mechanical I just won't let it go until I've solved the problem. And if I can't find the answer then I'll just use lots of big, difficult words to describe it.

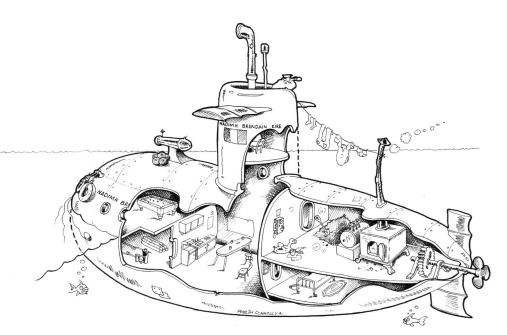

There's only one person in the world who shares my *Boys Own* passion for engines, and it's certainly not my wife. Joe Taylor is an actor and a contributor to the show. He is a great creative force, without whose input the programme would be nowhere near as exciting as it is. But when the work is done he often comes back to the house in Clontarf if he's got a new book on a submarine or a battleship.

I suppose growing old is the ultimate challenge. There's no answer to that one. You just get on with it and live life to the full. After all, nobody could have told Gay twenty-five years ago that he'd be Ireland's No. 1 broadcaster in the Nineties. Back then no one knew what this country would be like in a quarter of a century. It certainly hasn't grown old. If anything, it has grown up.

It's always been worth it

Old age doesn't scare me. Not on the radio. I don't know about television or any other form of entertainment but radio is the one area that defies fashion, style and age. Of all the avenues I choose to take – the choices that are now wide open to me as a result of the success of the programme – I can see myself doing radio until the day I drop. That's because it's worth it.

It's always been worth it.

Terence

Terence beamed in to planet Earth twenty-eight years ago and skidded to a halt at the Bon Secours Maternity Hospital in Cork. 'Never mind, love, we can go again for the boy,' were his father's opening remarks. Why providence had chosen Cork, Ter's dad could never understand. 'Why us?' he was heard to mutter as the perplexed parents drove home from hospital with the bespectacled blonde baby in the back seat of their Ford Anglia. But Terence's mother somehow knew that one day her ugly duckling would blossom and become a drake.

All I wanted to do was dance

'Me Dad wanted me to play hurlin' for Cork, but sure, all I wanted to do was dance.' The situation came to a head one slate-grey November evening when Ter and Mam were watching *Murphy agus a Chairde* on the box while soaking their feet in two dishes of salted water. 'Me Dad just grunted, got up, went out to buy de *Echo* to see if dere was anyone dead belongin' to us, and never came back again. 'Twas all my fault, I s'pose, but sure he's happy now, livin' in a kip and workin' on de buildings in London. He often writes home for money. It's just his little way of lettin' us know dat he still cares.'

Schooldays were hard. *Sin amach do lamh* was the first smidgeon of Irish that Terence learned from the Brothers. But he's quite philosophical about the experience. 'I suppose I drove 'em to it. I mean when the blood pressure goes up, dey had to go with it or dey'd burst.'

The schoolyard was harder still, especially when Todger Ryan, the school bully, would use Ter's face to break paving slabs for missiles to throw at the girls from the convent. 'Ah, Todger was a gas man,' says Terence. No girls were allowed in the gang, especially when they played Robin Hood. Todger was always Robin, Hawker played Little John, Slasher became the wicked Sheriff of Nottingham and Terence was Maid Marian. 'Well, someone had to do it and I didn't

Terence as 'Lawrence of Las Palmas', sharing some shamrock with Gerry in the Canaries over Patrick's weekend, 1991.

mind really, except when de Sheriff tied me to a tree and all de other kids threw worms at me.'

A degree in spelling

Apart from a degree in spelling, most of Terence's academic seeds were, like his face in the schoolyard, thrown on barren ground. His Leaving Cert. yielded two honours, Domestic Science and Irish Dancing. So the lovable Leesider turned his sights on the labour market. His original choice of career was Bob-a-Job. 'Yerra, when de decimal currency came in I got confused and chucked it in. After a few weeks I got a start in de hairdressin' trade.'

But seven years into his apprenticeship, the hapless Ter was still 'out de back doin' the towels', except when there was a rush on and he was summoned to give a hand in the ship. 'I might be let have a go on some ould fella, now like, who was goin' a bit bald maybe and who wouldn't have too much feelin' in his head.'

Once he applied too much setting lotion to a lady customer's hair. The resulting concrete coiffure almost lead to court proceedings. But Terence managed to convince her that the crash-helmet look was all the rage this year. 'Another satisfied customer,' says Ter.

It was while working in the salon, or saloon as Terence calls it, that he first made contact with the Ryan Line. He would ring Gerry to proffer advice to listeners in distress and to assure them that 'we're all God's children'. 'Before I knew it, I had so many people crying on my shoulder that I got rheumatism in me shoulder pads.' So when Terence was accused of theft and ignominiously relieved of his position, it was only natural that Gerry should offer him the role of agony uncle to the nation.

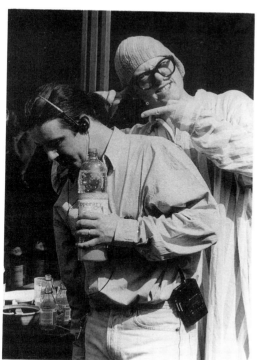

Terence sneaks up on Gerry during the Show's live Garden Party for 'People in Need' Day, May 1990.

'Fired? I was thrun out on me ear! Mrs Cussens came in for a wash and blow-dry. Because she's very old and hasn't a bob to her name, I only charged her £1.50. De gaffer threw a wobbler and called me a tief. I apologised and tried to put some of me own money in de till. Mrs Cussens started cryin' and de quare fella man-handled me in front of all de customers and told me never to darken his door-step again. I'm still not de better of it,' he says with quivering voice.

71

A Star if Born

In April 1989 a female caller suggested he release a record for the People in Need Fund. Never one to shun a challenge, the bould Ter went straight to work, even though his voice was breaking at the time. Willie O'Reilly, then producer of *The Gerry*

Terence as pop star, recording 'Que Sera Sera' with Maxi and Gerry, 1988.

Que Sera Sera *Ryan Show*, enlisted the help of record producer Denis Woods and distributor Dave Pennefeather. Windmill Lane Studios offered their services. With the help of backing vocalists Maxi, Gerry, Barbara and Brenda, *Que Sera Sera* was born, and all the money went to the People in Need Fund.

Terence's first public appearance was at the National Stadium on the night of the Telethon. As Paul Brady, Mary Coughlan, the Hothouse Flowers and Def Leppard re-grouped on stage for the Grand Finale, the 2,000-strong crowd had another star in mind. 'Terence! Terence! Terence!' they chanted. The estranged hairdresser from Cork duly obliged with a verse of that week's chart topper: *Que Sera Sera.*

'Yerra, I was glad to do it. I mean, I used to be a people in need myself once.'

I gets on great with Gay Watkins Soon, offers of public appearances were flooding in, and even when they weren't, he showed up anyway. 'I even went to de Rose of Tralee, to introduce de Roses on de telly from de Dome, but dey said I couldn't do it coz I wasn't gay! Actually I gets on great with Gay Watkins. He even had me on de *Late Late* which was a great honour, except I missed de

Doris Day film on Network 2 as a result. He sang *Que Sera Sera* with meself and Gerry and we were all holding hands. It was a great night except me Mam got a bit carried away with de Buckfast Abbey Tonic Wine in the Hostility Room backstage.'

In contrast, Terence is a teetotaller himself. 'Dat's right, love, I don't drink nor smoke really, except of an occasion like a weddin' or somethin'. I might have a glass of Babycham and a Consulate, y'know, just to be sociable, like!' Generally he confines his social life to helping with the local meals on wheels, 'de old timers are gas and dey love an oul' chinwag', and he enjoys an occasional game of bingo at the Glen Hall. 'I never won nothin' but I got a sweet once.'

Theological Ter!
'Me Mam is fierce holy altogether,' says Ter. 'I'm no pagan myself. I watches the Angelus and sez me prayers, like.' When he was a little lad, he lived in fear of the saints manifesting themselves in his bedroom at night. 'I used to keep a little torch under de bedclothes in case St Finbarr would show up with a message for de world. But I'm all right now except for limbo.' Why limbo, I probed. 'Well, one minute it was dere, like, and next minute dey got rid of it. I hope someone told de little babies. I mean we don't want dem floating out dere for eternity, do we?

'I often goes down to 9 o'clock Mass with me Mam and Mrs Cussens. Yesterday we went to an economical service and it was lovely.' Economical? Surely he meant Ecumenical? 'No, love, economical. Dey never sent de plate around.'

The Last Temptation of Terence
2FM Chaplain Fr Brian D'Arcy was sent for when Terence thought he might have a priestly vocation. The Padre suggested the lad spend seven days of quiet reflection away from the pressures of showbusiness. So a few days later, through the magic of an mobile phone, *The Gerry Ryan Show* faithful heard of his progress. From the mountaintop forest at Gougane Barra, near the Cork/Kerry border, came a faint voice: 'Yes, Ger, I can just hear you. I'm exhausted from draggin' me suitcases around de wilderness. I'm **Grizzly Adams without de grizzle** living on roots and berries and me moral is very low. I'm like Grizzly Adams without de grizzle.'

'I'm glad you're following in the footsteps of St Francis of Assisi', enthused the Great Beardless One.

'Followin' in St Francis' footsteps, is it? Well, if I catch up with him, I'll tell him you called him a sissy!' shouted the voice on the other end of the fading telephone line.

GER: 'That's not what I meant – has there been any manifestation from Heaven, a sign perhaps?'

TER: 'Yes, dere was a sign dis mornin'.'

GER: 'What form did it take?'

TER: 'It said: "Kenmare 11 miles".'

'I give up,' sighed Gerry.

'Ger, will you (crackle) tell me Mam dat I (crackle) . . . 'ove her and dat (crackle) . . . (beep).'

'TER! COME IN, Ter!'

For days *The Gerry Ryan Show* failed to raise the missing hermit as he continued his search for Life's unanswered questions, such as: 'Who am I?

Gerry pleads with Terence!

Where do I belong? What gas mark for baked alaska? And is there life after death? . . . ' Then, out of the blue . . .

GER: 'What's that? Terence has been eating wild mushrooms, and he's on the line? Quick! Put him through! Hello, Ter Lad. Are you all right?'

TER: 'Is dat you, Mam?'

GER: 'No, it's Gerry.'

TER: 'Gerry who?'

GER: 'Oh no! Please Ter, listen to me. YOU-ARE-IN-GREAT-DANGER. Tell us where you are!'

TER: 'I'm here . . . (crackle) . . . goodbye (beep).'

When the Air Corps helicopter finally found him, he was in an even more deranged state than usual. Two days later, from his sick bed, the boy wonder revealed that the wild mushrooms had played tricks on his mind.

The Vatican heaved a sigh of relief 'Well, y'know, I eats nothing with a face, but I was starved and I saw dis lamb in de next field. Lambo Ryan told me all about his rock in de sock escapade so I put a pebble into one of me anklets and swung it over me head. Just as I was about to bring it down on his little head, de lamb spoke to me: "St Terence, St Terence of de Wireless", sez he. "Yes", sez I. "Leave dis place and go forth." (Dat was very good for me coz I usually comes fifth or even last.) Anyway, go forth to de city of Cork, sez he, and look after your mudder and solve de problems of your nation, for derein lies your true vocation. So be off with you now before I set de dogs on ye.'

So the would-be cleric decided he wouldn't be, and the Vatican heaved a sigh of relief.

Whose house is it anyway?

The boy wonder and his mater live in a modest two-up two-down in Cork's arty quarter. 'Well, dere's a framing shop up de road a bit.'

On a recent tour of their habitat, I was treated to a rare glimpse of how the other half lives. The predominant shades are pale pink and rich mustard, a novel if somewhat nauseating combination which might well be the source of Terence's occasional bouts of depression.

'Dis is de livin' room,' he says enthusiastically. 'Note our prize-winning collection of ornaments.' One couldn't possibly disregard the motley assemblage of bric-a-brac. On the mantelpiece alone were a porcelain leaping trout (a souvenir of Birr, Co. Offaly), a picture of Terence as an altarboy, a pair of flamenco dancers from their trip to the Canary Islands, a plastic nodding cow from the back of Uncle Jerry's Morris Oxford, an ashtray from Butlins, a toy donkey complete with baskets of turf, and the piece to test your resistance: 'a roundy little glass ting full of water with a cottage inside, dat snows when you shake it.'

Pale pink and rich mustard The theme is carried throughout. The kitchen dresser proudly displays an extensive selection of jams and marmalades from the Iarnrod Eireann dining car. In the hall there hangs a gold disc for *Que Sera Sera* and beside it a framed wedding photograph of Mam and Dad, which is now turned to face the wall.

The bathroom houses a Beleek jug from the Eucharistic Congress of 1932 and bath towels taken in error from Jury's Hotel by Ter's father. 'Oops!' he says as he hastily ushers me out of the bathroom and back downstairs. 'We're not quite finished doin' up de bathroom yet,' he says defensively, 'but what did you tink of our new shower? It saves us having to boil pots of water to fill de bath tub in de back kitchen. Mind you, de shower was nearly de death of me de day we got it put in. I was havin' a grand oul rub-a-dub-dub when dere was a ring at de doorbell. "Mam", sez I. "Get that love, willya Mam?" But she was sound asleep in her rockin' chair. So I just shouted out de window: "I'm in the shower. Who is it?" A voice from below said: "It's just the blind man." Fair enough, sez I to myself, I'll chance it. So I ran downstairs with no clothes on to give him a few bob. "Right," sez he when I opened de door, "where would you like your blinds put?" I scarpered up de stairs to protect me modesty.'

We finished our tour in Ter's boudoir where the Christmas crib was already in place. 'It's not great, really', he admits. 'You see, all de figures come from different sets and dat explains why St Joseph is twice as big as de donkey.' I declined an invitation to examine the ornaments on the sideboard in the drawing room and bade him farewell. Ah well! Beauty is in the eye of the beholder.

A simple lad

Despite his star status, Terence likes the simple things in **I eats nothin' with a face** life. For example, he is a latter-day vegetarian. 'I eats nothin' with a face. I mean, I might eat an egg all right but nothin' with a face, not even an oul sardine. Me favourite dish is de Terence Mixed Grill.' The Terence Mixed Grill? I enquired. 'Yes, love. It's simple really, boiled potatoes, roast potatoes, chips, and mash.' The Egon Ronay of the south has also inherited his mother's sweet tooth and once ate twelve Cadbury's Creme Eggs and a large tin of pears at a sitting.

Parking spaces are always at a premium in the southern capital, so the former hairdresser's preferred mode of transport is his trusty rusty moped. ''Tis as old as de hills, a 1962 Kamikaze 50 wot me Uncle Jerry swapped me for two Julie Andrews records and a box of old *Sunday Worlds*.'

The poor lad almost came a cropper once or twice. On one occasion, he was rushing to finish his meals on wheels run when disaster struck. 'I was leggin' it, comin' round a corner, doin' at least 25 mph when one of me stabilisers fell off. I went flyin' across de road, hit a crow right between the eyes and knocked meself senseless. I was in an awful state. I wanted to report it to de proper authorities but I couldn't trace de owner of de crow.'

Considering the lad doesn't shave, he's had a few close ones. 'Tell it to Terence,' his weekly half-hour agony column, experienced intermittent technical problems.

'It's all right, Ger. Our technical man Finbarr is here helpin' me sort it out,' he says reassuringly.

Getting in the mood at the start of Gerry's show from the Canaries, March 1991.

'Be careful, Ter,' warns Gerry.

'It's okay, I'm just holding dese two wires here while Finbarr plugs dem in to see which one is faul . . . AAARRGH . . . AAH . . . AAH . . .'

'Terence, are you all right, old buddy?' Gerry asks in panic, but there's no reply from Cork. He tries again. 'Finbarr, if you're there, for God's sake, do something!'

'What can I do? Sure he's leppin' around like a fish on a bank,' screeches the sparkless electrician over the staccato yelping coming from the trembling heap on the floor beside him.

'For pity's sake, man, give him the kiss of life!'

'Y'mean, ya want me to give Terence the kiss of life? Not on your nelly!'

A week later, the slightly over-cooked juvenile lead of *The Gerry Ryan Show* was back on the air from his hospital bed. 'Well, I'm out of de coma now, I tink, Gerry. All I remember was an almighty bang and a smell of burning rashers as me

Me eyebrows flew off and de studio caught fire

eyebrows flew off and de studio caught fire. Most of me memory has been erased as well.'

'You're not missing much,' assures Gerry.

'Did I always have an Afro hairstyle?' continues Ter as Dr Watt, the burns specialist, explains his somewhat unorthodox treatment.

'Yes, Gerry, as soon as his hair is straightened we'll continue draining the residual electricity from his body.'

'Will that hurt the poor lad?' enquires Gerry.

'Not at all,' promises the Doc. 'He's wired up through a series of cables to a collection of tractor headlamps, high-powered bulbs and fairy lights. When the last fairy light dims and goes out, we'll know he's clear of any remaining current and it won't be long before we're rid . . . I mean, before he's back on his feet again.'

Romantic confusion It was around this time that Terence met Bridie from the local library. 'Yes,' he enthuses, 'she's thirty-eight and an orphan with no family except for Donal, her goldfish.' But how did they meet, I probed.

'Well, I answered her ad in de *Farmers Journal* and she answered mine in *Ireland's Own*. So we met outside de Savoy on Friday night and outside Easons on de Saturday. I didn't know what was happening – I thought she was two-timin' me or somethin'. It's all new to me.' So this was his first crush then?

'Ah God, no. Me first crush was up behind de goal when Cork scored de winner in de 1976 Munster Final.'

'Yes, but was Bridie his first romantic encounter', I continued.

'No, I fell in love with a nice girl from Bandon once. I even proposed to her but her family were dead set against it.' Her family, I queried? 'Yes, y'know, her husband and three children.'

Left to right: Terence, Nita Byrne, Gerry, Barbara Jordan, Siobhain Hough in the Canaries, March 1991.

Despite all this romantic confusion, Bridie and her beau are getting on like a studio on fire and she never charges Terence the penny a day fine when he's late returning his mother's Mills & Boon books to the library.

'We went to de Canary Islands with Gerry and de crew for St Patrick's Day but dat was a disaster. I was bringing shamrock through Customs and when asked if it was grass, I said yes it's Irish Grass. I was frogmarched away by de Guardia Civil, who weren't too civil to me, I can tell you.'

The authorities sent the shamrock off for analysis and after a brief interview they decided to send the boy broadcaster off for analysis as well. The shamrock passed and Terence failed.

So what does the future hold for Terence: a Jacob's Award perhaps? 'I'd be lucky to get a Club Milk,' he quips. 'I just want to be happy and cheer up people who aren't because we're all God's children.'

But what about the people closest to him? 'He's a real sweetie,' claims his fiancée, Bridie. 'On my birthday, he showed up with a box of Irish Roses. He actually bought two boxes, picked out all my favourites and put them into the box he gave me.'

Gerry Ryan maintains the lad is too highly strung for his own good. 'That fella is so tense, if he relaxes it makes him nervous. Otherwise he has a heart of gold and loves to help people less well off than himself.'

His mother has the last word, as always. 'I blame his father,' she says. **'Grow up, stupid!'** 'When Ter was a lad, his father would regularly give him a clip behind the ear and say, "Grow up, stupid!" and I s'pose he did.'

THE BLACK
SWIRL...

GRAVITY .. ..

LEVITY .. ..

Brenda...

Report from a sewer

'Are you in yet?' he said to me.

'No I'm not,' I said. 'What d'you think I am – a dwarf?'

'Well, either you squeeze into those overalls or you'll be covered in shit from head to toe.'

'Oh.' Somehow I managed to squeeze into the overalls. They were meant for a child, I was convinced of that. Though why a child would want to work down a sewer for a living was a total mystery.

But people work in sewers, just as I know people work on radio shows. Unfortunately, in my case, the two jobs just happened to run into each other one night 100 feet below the streets of Dublin.

It's my own bloody fault, I suppose. After all, I was the one to suggest going down there in the first place.

'Hey,' I said at a programme meeting one afternoon. 'I know! Why don't I do a report from a sewer. It'd be great.' The meeting stopped dead in its tracks. Everyone looked at me. They had been discussing the risks of Gerry cycling into work in the first hour of the show the next day to see how long it would take, compared to using a car. Then I butt in with a totally different topic.

They were dying to explode with laughter. I could see it on each one of their faces. But somehow the producer kept his cool and just smiled.

'Hmmmm, yes. A sewer report. I suppose there's something in that. Yeah. A sewer. Hmmm. And, eh, when do you think you could do it?' he asked me.

'Any time. Now, if you want.' I knew they thought I was nuts. They were probably right. I rang the Corporation. They thought I was nuts as well. But they gave me permission, all the same.

I was well aware it was a crazy idea. But crazy moments like this are always welcome on *The Gerry Ryan Show*. In fact I was surprised no one had thought of it before. Sometimes the best ideas on the show turn out to be the ones staring you straight in the face.

The bowels of the city

I met the man who was assigned as my guide to the bowels of the city. In the right suit he could have been a business man on the Stock Exchange. He didn't look dirty, he didn't smell. He was the complete opposite of what I had expected an engineer, with the city's sewer department to look like.

'Are you sure you want to do this?' he asked me, scratching his head as if suddenly some link in his logic had just walked out the door.

'Sure I'm sure,' I replied, with my eyes full

Fat Men...

It was a hot balmy summer's day in May 1990. Gerry had just finished talking to a woman who had developed her own personal organiser for pregnant women. The pop singer Suzanne Vega was due in studio any moment for an interview. But first there was a call from a man with a weighty problem.

Michael Day was over eighteen stone. He was talking from the cabin of his truck which he drove along the length and breadth of Ireland and Europe. His

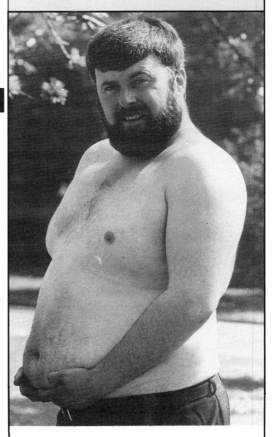

Michael Day weighs in at the start of his diet.

Fat Men cont........

weight was getting to him. The cramped conditions of his cab and his colossal bulk were making him sweat. He wanted to shed the flab, and fast. His plight quickly caught the attention of the male population of Ireland, many of whom, it is well known, are themselves overweight. Michael pledged that he would do everything in his power to lose the pounds. And Gerry promised to follow his exploits every few weeks into the summer.

Not long after that Martin O'Reilly phoned Gerry to say he would undertake the same challenge and would report back to the show with his progress. He, too, was eighteen stone. He, too, drove a van. So together both men spent most of their day on their behinds with little room for exercise and lots of time for snacks. This was going to be the mother of all challenges.

Soon after the day's programme Michael Maher, a dietitian, phoned the office to say he was prepared to help both men with a specially prepared diet. Producer Joan Torsney decided to bring all three men to the studio the following week to officially launch the big adventure. The deadline would be the last show of the season before Gerry went on holidays, on 20 July.

'Losing a stone in a fortnight isn't going to work long term. What we're talking about is losing weight over a prolonged period of time,' Michael Maher explained. The two men joined him in the studio. It was true. They *were* big.

'Gerry, what I'm worried about is, will my skin hang down like a rhinoceros after I've lost all this weight? Will it be hanging down off me?' Michael

of burning ambition and drive but my mind beginning to show signs of abandoning ship. I moulded the rest of my body into those tiny overalls.

'Now get that jacket on, and then the helmet,' he said handing me the gear. There was dried-in dirt and muck glued rigidly to the material of the jacket. The gloves were the wrong fit too, only this time they were far too big.

'Have you any protective cover for your recording machine?' he asked pointing to the portable recorder sitting on the bonnet of my car.

'Oh no!' I shrieked. 'What'll I do?' He looked at me as if I was a little child dying to go for a wee wee. Well, I'd obviously come to the right place for that.

'Just hold it close to you and take your chances,' he said. 'Come on. Switch on your lamp. You'll need it down there.'

We walked over to the manhole. We were on a street next to the Liffey, across the river from the civic offices at Wood Quay. I looked like a coal miner coming off shift. But the furthest I'd been below ground was when I dug a hole on a beach and jumped into it.

Then it hit me. Right between the nasal passages. I felt as if my knees were going to give way as the power of the whiff threw its first reeling punch. Wow. That was smelly.

My parents won't like *this* report, I thought as I watched the man climb down the ladder into the darkness and the smell. They had been so proud of me when they heard my delicate voice on the radio for the first time. I started out doing small, funny reports on events around the country as well as movie reviews. I was fresh out of college with a degree and the real world greeting me with friendly outstretched arms.

Gerry sounded so fresh on the radio. No scripts, no set-ups, no stale air. I knew this show had a different appeal. The people working behind the scenes were prepared to take chances. So after a couple of weeks of regular reports I began to add a few ideas of my own. You never know what you're capable of unless you chance your arm.

One day at a meeting I said I wanted to do an interview with a trans-sexual for the show. This was new territory. Nothing like this had been heard on daytime radio. And,

Martin O' Reilly weighs in at the start of his diet.

Fat Men cont........

Day asked. Gerry reassured him, telling him not to worry and to plough on.

The two men got back in their cabs and travelled into the unknown. The show followed them with regular calls on their epic quest for a slimmer frame. Michael Day gave up sugar.

'And all the sugar I should have used I put into a plastic bag. At the end of the week, Gerry, I had one kilo of sugar.'

Martin explained his daily routine, a schedule that seemed to revolve around nothing but food.

'I used to eat around 3,400 calories a day. I used to eat close to one and a half loaves of bread a day, about five to six spuds and chocolate. But now I'm down

84

to four slices of bread and two spuds per day. It's getting better.'

Their updates inevitably drew more calls on the subject. The calls came from as far as Liverpool, where one listener reckoned their size was a problem of the mind and not of the stomach. But the men continued to stick with the diet despite the pressures.

'The first fortnight was a living hell,' says Michael. 'Gerry, it was a prison sentence.'

Both men went through periods of depression, according to Michael Maher. That is when most people simply give up. But Michael told them to ring him whenever they felt tempted by the occasional whiff of a bacon sandwich, the grease dripping off the edges of the bread like treacle off a spoon.

In July Michael and Martin weighed in on *The Gerry Ryan Show*. There was a sense of triumph in their voices as they proudly announced to the world that they were winning. The fat was falling off them. They no longer felt like sardines in a tin can when they got into the cabins of their lorries. But they weren't going to stop there.

'I want to be on Dollymount Beach in August, Gerry,' said Michael, 'in a pair of swimming shorts and I don't want to be going round with a pair of tits on me like a woman.'

Gerry added his own proof of the pudding.

'Apparently his libido has improved. That's a polite word for his mickey.'

Martin was happy to say that his waist measurement had gone from 44 to 42 inches. Even that in itself was a victory. He was able to fit into a suit he'd bought many years before and he wasn't about to give up that pleasure for any jam butty.

while I didn't have a lot of experience of doing interviews, they said they were willing to give it a try. Looking back, at the time we were all trying to find out how far the show could go. This would be a test.

A week later, much to my parents' surprise there was Brenda on the air, interviewing a man who desperately wanted to be a woman. I remember some of the phone calls of revulsion and horror from listeners who heard this man talk about his life as a woman in the wrong sex. To me it wasn't revolting. It was just very sad. He had been nervous about doing the interview. But he had a drink to steady the nerves and to me he came across as a very human person in a frightening situation. That report was the shape of things to come for me on *The Ryan Show*. That was the summer of 1988. We were all trying to find our feet.

But now I wasn't so sure of my path ahead as I put those feet on the first slippery step of the ladder leading me down into this hole. If hell had toilets for its guests then it couldn't be worse than this. The man was looking up at me from his squelchy standpoint way down below. He told me to take my time. With the smell coming up at me like a gust of farts the only thing I was thinking of taking was my leave.

My foot slipped once. This was going to be ugly. I just knew it. I inched my way down with my tape recorder under my arm and a microphone around my neck.

'You're nearly there. Just one more step and you're there.'

Fat Men cont........

The final day arrived. The show had moved out of its dark studio setting in the basement at Montrose. Instead, the team had set up camp in the beautiful surrounds of Adare Manor on the other side of the country. The first classical music festival was taking place at the manor and Gerry decided to pay them a visit for the final show before he took a well-earned rest. Michael Day said he'd be able to travel for the day. But nobody could contact Martin. He was nowhere to be found. It looked as if only one contestant would be able to weigh in on the morning.

It was a hot sunny day as the guests poured in during the morning's show. They

I stepped down on to the surface of the sewer. I felt like Neil

I felt like Neil Armstrong

Armstrong when he took his first few steps on the surface of the moon. I only wish I had his space suit and breathing apparatus. I didn't know which was worse for my body – to breathe through my nose or my mouth.

The

Slime everywhere

place looked like what I'd imagine the small intestine of an animal to look like. There was slime everywhere, oozing out of every part of the wall, from top to bottom. I'm glad I didn't suffer from claustrophobia. The tunnel was small. In order to walk we had to keep our heads stooped low. No wonder the Phantom of the Opera lived in a sewer. These tunnels were custom-made for tales of horror. I held on to my

Fat Men cont........

included gossip columnist Terry Keane and Zig and Zag. Across the river from the manor a team of heavy earth-moving machines, which were levelling the countryside for a new golf course, took the morning off at the manor's expense to bring back the peace and silence of a rural atmosphere.

Michael Day was a happy man. A guest of the show and the proud owner of a slimmer frame. He finished off just below seventeen and a half stone. A loss of just over a stone.

'I couldn't have done it without you, Gerry,' he gratefully admitted. It seemed such a shame that Martin was not there for the final count.

The show was winding up. There were just ten minutes left before Gerry went on his hols and the final item of the show, a musical group, was getting ready to rock. Then out of the crowds came Martin with a smile on his face and his family on his arm.

'Sorry I didn't get here sooner,' he said. He had taken his holidays, completely forgetting that they coincided with the final weigh-in. And besides, he had firmly resolved to go on losing the flab, long beyond his deadline.

'But when I heard Gerry on the radio saying this was the last show I just turned the car around and raced over to Adare. It was only luck that I happened to be in the area.' Martin's weight was just under seventeen stone. Another big slice off the belly.

For both men the hard work and discipline had paid off. They were happier, healthier people and agreed the best way to lose weight was slowly but surely.

Their story on *The Ryan Show* ended that day. But the flab-fight went on behind

tape recorder as if my life depended on it. I felt almost sorry for bringing it down into these depths. I had brought it with me on many different travels, but this was the worst. In those early days the tape recorder was the main link between Gerry's studio and the outside world.

A lot of the time back then Barbara and I did vox pops for the show, where we would ask people on the streets for their opinions and thoughts on everything, from how to care for your granny to where you'd most like to make love. (It's amazing how many people like a quick screw in the kitchen before dinner.)

One time Gerry was discussing the national anthem. Very few people he talked to knew the words of the anthem. So I was told to go out and record a couple of people who said they knew the words. I guess I got a little over-enthusiastic. I came back with practically half the nation singing their hearts out. Reports on tape were only supposed to be about three minutes maximum. It took them days to edit my one down. I wasn't sent on a vox pop for weeks after that.

There were a number of times when I went to interview someone in particular and found to my horror when I got back that the batteries were dead and the interview had to be done all over again. But there was one time I made sure I had everything on tape.

The Virgin Mary

I went to Wexford to interview two women who claimed to have seen visions of the Virgin Mary. I turned up in time to see them in the throes of another trance. There was pandemonium at the church where this was taking place. The crowd was getting bigger all the time and surging towards the women. The atmosphere was spiced with a mixture of fear and excitement. I didn't know what to believe. The women remained in that trance for another twenty minutes. I moved through the

Fat Men cont........
the scenes. Michael was satisfied with his loss and couldn't thank the show enough at his lettuce dinner in Adare later that day. Martin, however, continued to lose the pounds for many weeks after the show. He got down to just above sixteen stone and still gets regular check-ups from Michael Maher.

Not surprisingly, Michael Maher has been getting a steady stream of people looking for advice on their weight ever since the saga of the fat men took place.

Brenda testing 'Body Wrap' technique to purify the skin and lose inches, September 1990.

huge gathering with my tape recorder, asking people what they felt was happening. Some seemed sure this was a real visitation from the Virgin Mary, but most admitted they hadn't got a clue what was going on, but that it was exciting all the same.

I hung around the church once it was all over. The women remained inside the church. They seemed genuine enough and appeared to have come through some sort of experience, whatever it was. They joined the priest inside for a chat. The crowd was breaking up and going home. The long line of cars that dotted the countryside was beginning to disappear. The priest asked the two women when the Virgin Mary would be returning to them.

'At seven o'clock, this day, next week,' they both replied.

The priest remained silent in thought for a few moments. Then he looked them both straight in the eye and said quietly: 'She couldn't pay us a visit at half past seven, could she? We'd have more time to settle the crowd then, you see.'

The two girls agreed on the new time.

Kept a diary At that moment a tall, bulky man pointed to me in the church and shouted, 'Have you got that tape recorder switched on?' I said no, and left the place soon after. I knew this country had seen many visions of the Virgin Mary, but it was the first time I'd recorded proof that she kept a diary.

It's all Barbara's fault, of course. She brought me into the show in the first place. If it wasn't for her I'd probably be earning a 'clean' living in an office somewhere. But trust her to open her big mouth one day when the show was looking for somebody new. I bet you she got a few brownie points for that.

We get on okay in the office, I suppose, except she's got a bigger desk and likes to spread out all her letters and notebooks to make it look like she's

Brenda as fairy godmother in Henry Street, December 1990.

89

Makes You Think

Just when you least expect it a call comes into the show that leaves both listeners and Gerry riveted to the spot.

In September 1990 a woman phoned in to the show to make a comment about hospitals. Her father had died recently in a hospital ward. Nothing unusual in that except she had a very simple question to ask. Her voice began to break as the words came out.

'Why ... why don't they have a place ... a quiet room even ... for people like my father to die in. To die with dignity.

'They knew he was going to die. They told me a few hours before that there was no hope for him. We knew he was going, and we had to sit next to him, in a public ward, with other patients and doctors and nurses whizzing around.

'I wanted to talk to my father. I wanted to tell him things I've wanted to tell him all my life. But I couldn't. I just couldn't ... not there, not in the middle of all that. And he died ... that was my last chance to talk to him ... and he died.'

Gerry didn't talk. He left the line open, and in her own time she continued.

'I'm not blaming anybody. The doctors did their best. We knew he was going to die. But if only a hospital could give people a place to go to, a place where my father could have died with dignity and with his family.'

Her call received many wishes of sympathy. In many ways, after a call like hers, the rest of a programme seems pointless. The only thing to do in that case is play music and let people think about it for themselves for a while.

Early in 1991 the topic of transvestism dropped into the programme without any warning. A man phoned in to talk about his life as a transvestite, a life that he had given up for the sake of his wife. She didn't know he had worn women's clothes and met men with similar desires. And he never wanted her to know. So he put his past behind him. His descriptions and his feelings proved very powerful on the air.

It also provoked many calls, among which was a woman who told Gerry she was married to a transvestite. And she knew of his other world. In fact, it was quite an open secret.

'To try and keep him in men's clothes and women's clothes is very expensive. I'll be in town with him and I'll be buying something for myself and I'll say do you fancy something in here?'

She was very nervous, and to hide her fears she laughed under her breath from time to time. But there was no hiding the reality of her situation.

'There's no easy way to tell a woman that her husband is a transvestite. We were married ten years and I can remember finding underwear hid behind the immersion.

'I love my husband very much.'

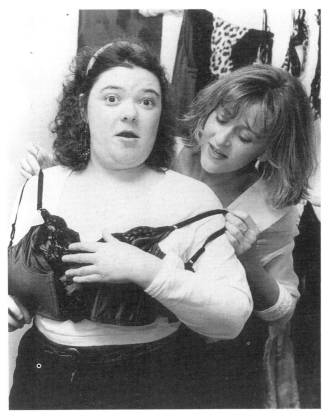

working. But although she's a terrible fusspot on the job and she never takes enough clean knickers with her when we're travelling abroad, she's pretty good fun to work with, especially when we're on a story together.

It's bad enough when one of us goes on a report, but when the 'Two Bs' hit the streets you'd better watch out. Nothing stands in our way, whether we're begging or busking or even farming together.

Brenda in lingerie shop, being fitted, November 1990.

Makes You Think cont........

She described how he would sit in the same room as her dressed in women's underwear. Sometimes he might put on a dress. Gerry asked her how she felt.

'I do want to laugh, personally because to see a man in women's underwear is hilarious. He has a good body, well built, not perfect but I'm happy with him. But I wouldn't laugh. That'd be the worst thing to do.'

The strength in her love for her husband stood out like a beacon. She was very brave to talk about such things. She said she hoped she was coming to terms and coping with her husband's life.

'But he still feels guilty,' said Gerry.

'He still feels guilty. He'd say, you don't like me doing this, sure you don't, and I'll say, no I don't, and at the same time I'm thinking, Jesus, if you only knew how stupid you looked. I'm as confused as he is.

'Very, very slowly I think I've learned to accept it better. I mean I've walked along the Liffey saying I'll throw myself in, I just can't accept it, I'm so alone.

91

It's always good to have the other 'B' on the case, even if she does try to steal all the limelight! At least I'm a better singer.

My sewer guide took some delight in telling me the sort of things they come across in the murky depths of the city's sewerage system.

'It's just amazing what people flush down their loos,' he said. He sounded as if he was describing the origins of the universe. The one good thing is the size of the rats. They're not super rats as legend would tell us. The radio-reporter-eating rat is as fictitious as pizza-crazed turtles in the sewers of Manhattan.

But there are plenty of sanitary towels and condoms as well as the less flushable items on the list, like knickers, socks, jewellery, wallets, cash and even a toupé on one occasion. I kept my eyes glued to the surface of the stream as we waded upriver. The stench was not getting any more bearable. The helmet came in very handy. The roof of the tunnel was low and

---

Makes You Think cont........

'Nobody knows how many times I've walked along that Liffey, to throw myself in. But it's not that easy when you've got children either, especially when you love your husband and he doesn't really understand you love him.'

She started to cry. Her story was over. Her life with her husband, however, goes on.

'I'm sorry.'

Gerry eased her out of her tears. She responded. She quietly joked with Gerry about how the only other bit of male company in the house was the family dog.

'I think you have done so extraordinarily well. It's a testament to the love that must obviously exist between the two of you, your commitment to your marriage, your commitment to your family, your commitment to your relationship. You are *so* strong and if you were here I'd give you the biggest hug that was humanly possible.'

'Oh, I love hugs.'

'And I've just been handed a piece of paper with a message. It reads: lots of calls from other women around the country who are in exactly the same position as you.'

'The only thing I'd say is that people give up so easily on their marriages. I'm not saying it's easy but... you just can't give up.'

'You said it, love. You're bloody right. You've spoken about what life is all about more eloquently and more genuinely than I've heard for a long time. You say you love him. Love him? You *are* him. Without you he would not exist.'

The calls of support rolled in for a long time after the show ended that day.

every now and then my head would hit off the ceiling disturbing the thick layer of slime that clung to the concrete wall. Tiny lumps of dirt would drop into the river below as if it had started to rain. My feet were freezing in their protective wellies. The rubber in them was so thin that sometimes I could feel little bumps under my feet. Everytime I felt one of these I let out a huge scream and lunged for my guide. They made for some great interruptions on the tape.

We roared across Europe

Working with a recorder means you always have a safety net. The tape can be edited and played at the right moment on the show. That's the way most radio shows work – a mixture of live chat and taped reports. But the fun really starts when the reports themselves are live instead of taped. And for that you need a mobile phone.

I was only on the show a couple of months when I was handed a mobile phone one day. I thought it was a walkie talkie. I had no idea what we were to do with it until I was told that we could phone live into Gerry's show from almost anywhere. It didn't take long before Barbara and I were using them every day on the show. And they've been our link for some of the wildest broadcasts I've ever done.

Like the time Barbara and I raced each other across Europe. We had two separate routes but the same destination: Athens. We roared across Europe for a week on the radio. Every day I'd phone the show on my mobile to give Gerry my location. Then I'd ask where Barbara was. He never gave me a straight answer so I never knew who was in the lead.

On the way out of Venice I called the show. Mobile phones sometimes don't work well on trains so I had to do the call standing next to my carriage only seconds before it was due to pull out of the station. I was live on the air telling everyone about my time in Venice, and all this time the station master, who hadn't a word of English, was trying to push me on to the train. I kept smiling at him and talking to Gerry. I nearly got arrested.

It was the most hectic week of my life. And on the final day of the race Gerry had one more trick up his sleeve. When both of us had made it to the finishing post in Athens he told us the race was not actually over yet.

'You've got to find a Mr Ramos at the Acropolis. Then phone me from there,' Gerry told us on the mobiles. Barbara and I looked at each other. We had just raced across Europe. We were hot, we were sweaty and we had two huge haversacks on our backs. If I'd had Gerry there at that moment I'd have told him to go get Mr bloody Ramos himself.

'Then you've got to race back to the finishing line and pick up a genuine Greek menu from any restaurant along the way.' We could have killed him.

I'll never forget those last hectic moments of the race to the Acropolis, or the 'Apocalypse' as I mistakenly called it. I jumped in a taxi and told the driver to get me to the tourist site as fast as he could go. I remember sitting in the back of the cab thinking there was just forty minutes to go to the end of the show back in Ireland. They had to have a winner in less than an hour.

As I raced up the giant concrete steps of the Acropolis I could have been climbing the stairs of a DART station in Dublin. The location didn't matter. What mattered was getting there in time. I was almost at the small tourist office where I would find my Mr Ramos when suddenly this heavy hand bore down on my shoulder. I thought I'd been nabbed by the Greek police.

'Outta my way!' 'Outta my way!' Barbara screamed as she tore past me. She was gone in a cloud of dust. But when I got to the office I nearly ran out of breath from laughing. There was Barbara, in this office, screaming for Mr Ramos. She might as well have been screaming for a pint of stout. There were four men in the office and not one of them knew what she was talking about. She just looked like some demented tourist who had finally seen one too many tourist attractions.

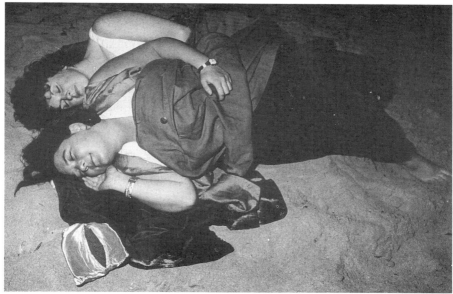

Barbara and Brenda asleep on the job, Europe 1990.

We never got to meet Mr Ramos. But we continued the race, picking up a Greek menu before getting to the winning post. I remember hopping out of the cab and rushing into the plush restaurant. There was no time for explanations in broken English. I just grabbed the menu and ran. In the end I wasn't fast enough. Barbara got there before me and won the race on the air with just five minutes to go before midday.

After the final call we both slumped down like two wrecks on the side of the road. There was a terrible sense of anti-climax. Nobody came up to us in the middle of Athens saying: 'Hey, Brenda, Barbara, I heard you on the show this morning.' How could anybody know. No one in Greece has ever heard of Gerry Ryan.

That's the great thing about doing reports at home. People are so willing to help. Most people know Gerry's show. So if they see me out on the streets with a mobile phone they will always oblige if I ask them for help or to go on the phone to talk to Gerry.

Once I had to do a report on what people think about when they're

Palermo...

With just one week to go to the start of the Italian World Cup an early indication of the type of madness the hosts could expect from the Irish arrived on the island of Sicily.

The Ryan Show team touched down in the capital of Palermo for a little on-side action of their own. They had travelled to Sicily to welcome Brenda and Barbara who were hitch-hiking across the mainland of Europe. Their destination was Palermo, and Gerry was going to be there to meet them, live on *The Ryan Show.*

Gerry was also about to meet one of the most extraordinary men ever to go on the programme. His name was Leoluca Orlando, the Mayor of Palermo and one of Italy's most outspoken critics of the Mafia regime.

Sicily is steeped in the myth of the Mafia. The Grand Hotel, where the team were guests, was originally the meeting place for the Sicilian criminal order as they planned their drug-trafficking invasion of the United States. The city police keep an armed guard on a number of apartment blocks dotted around Palermo. They are there to protect judges and high-ranking businessmen who defy the grip of the Mafia on the island's society.

The people try to lead ordinary lives. They desperately want to break with the old image of the machine gun in a violin case. And one of their most popular voices for the new generation is Mayor Orlando.

Gerry talking live to Leoluca Orlando, Mayor of Palermo in Sicily, May 1990.

Palermo cont........

Producer Paul Russell asked the Italian assistant assigned to the show about the possibility of an interview with the Mayor.

'Oh, I don't know. Mr Orlando is a very busy man. And, believe me, it takes much organisation for him to travel to the radio centre in Palermo,' she said. 'But I will try for you.'

Paul could only think of one reason why there would be such trouble about his visit. Paddy Agnew, an Irish journalist, had explained that the Mayor always travels in three cars. No one can tell which one he travels in as he changes cars each time. His bodyguards are in all of them. And when he steps out of his car the only sound you can hear is the click of guns as his guards release their safety catches. Mayor Orlando is a

on their bicycles. A new study had found that most cyclists spent their time thinking about sex. So I went on the streets to ask them. Usually there's a bit of time before the broadcast when I can ask people if they'd like to talk to Gerry. But that morning I hadn't any time at all and I was standing by ready to go on air as soon as the record faded.

Then on he comes and says 'Okay Brenda, where are you this morning?' I told him about the report and said I had gone into town that morning to ask cyclists what they thought about when they were on their bikes. And when Gerry said, 'Right Brenda, stop a cyclist there for us and we'll see what they think', I hadn't a soul lined up.

But sure enough I ran out on the streets, stopped a couple of cyclists and they all agreed to talk. Just like that. And while they were talking on the phone to the show I was stopping a few more.

And guess what? One of them admitted he'd been day-dreaming about sex. Now I'm not saying reporting is easy, but it does help when people are so obliging.

The streets are always full of stories. I prefer to

go searching for them rather than reading a good story in a newspaper in the office. I come across lots of unusual stories simply by spending a day in the city on my own.

One day I was in town to cover a party that was being held in a city centre hotel. On my way I dropped into the ladies' toilets on Stephens Green. Inside were two young girls leaning up against a sink and having a cigarette. I heard them talking about how little money they had. They were wearing school uniforms. I took the chance and asked them what they were doing in the toilets.

They were mitching from school. They weren't looking for an education. What they wanted was money and a man. I talked to them for a couple of minutes while women eyed us suspiciously as I shared a cigarette with them. I asked them what they liked to do when they were on the hop. They showed me. We walked down Grafton Street, looking at the shops and the boys. That's all they wanted to do.

The hotel wasn't very far away. I was about to leave the girls when both of them turned their heads, saying, 'Oh Jaysus'.

Palermo cont........

marked man. He never appears in public with his family. It is too dangerous. A former mayor who, it was learned, was about to inform on the Mafia was gunned down on the streets of Palermo. For Orlando to take a walk to the local shops is just pure suicide.

On the eve of the Sicilian show the team took time out to visit the sights. That really meant a slap-up meal and a pub crawl. They were accompanied by two members of the *Star* newspaper who were flown over to cover the show. There is a legend in the newspaper business that one of those members dipped another type of member into a glass of burning alcohol, for a dare. It simply isn't true. It wasn't a glass. It was an ashtray. The member in question didn't make another appearance during the stay in Palermo.

'You think that's bad?' Gerry explained to the barman. 'Wait 'till the Irish fans arrive in a few weeks time!'

Back at the hotel Paul found a message waiting for him.

'Mr Orlando would be honoured to go on Gerry's show. Please be ready for him at 11 a.m.'

The interpreters earned their medals the following day. None of the staff in the radio building spoke English. But when they discovered the Mayor was coming to visit them that morning the place went on red alert. You could hear station managers shouting from one floor to the next. The team didn't know what to expect. It was like waiting for a live drama to unfold.

Shortly before the agreed time the interpreter shouted: 'They're here.' Downstairs, like an echo of Paddy

Palermo cont........

Agnew's words, three large limousines drew up next to the building. A group of men jumped out and ran into the lobby. Within a few minutes a man appeared on the roof with a gun. At least two bodyguards were assigned to each floor.

They were big, brutish and thorough. Nothing was going to get through this wall of protection. Nobody on the show had ever seen anything like it, except in the movies. The adrenalin produced from working on a live chat show, particularly when it's coming from another country, was doubled with the arrival of this man.

And as yet he hadn't stepped out of the car.

Finally the command was given. The safety catches on their guns were released and Leoluca Orlando stepped out of the third car. He walked quickly up the stairs to the first floor and into Gerry's studio. A piece of music was playing as the two men shook hands.

Orlando was a modern man. Dressed stylishly and speaking fluent English, which he learned while in college in London in the Sixties, he carried himself confidently and breezed into the interview like a gust of fresh air. He explained how his life is dedicated to breaking the hold of the Mafia, and how each week he travels abroad to spread his word of change. But it's a tough battle, and whenever he has to move around the city his large family of guards move with him. Their very appearance in the radio building frightened the life out of the entire team. At any moment during Orlando's stay an attack on his life could have taken place. That attack would, no doubt, have included casualties around him. It wasn't a thought to dwell on.

'But please, Mr Ryan,' Orlando interrupted towards the end. 'Please let us not talk about the Mafia all the time. This island is not the Mafia's. It is the people's and they are young and full of life. We have much to offer to the world. So when you go home tell everyone that this island is a good place to visit.'

The guard at the studio door whistled. We heard the click once more as Orlando walked out the door. He shook hands with everyone and left. It felt as if the whole building breathed a sigh of relief.

'How could anybody do his job?' Gerry asked Paul as the guards slipped away. 'That's one type of fame I can do without.'

Both of their mothers were on the street and they spotted the girls. I stayed out of the way waiting for a furious row to break out. But the mothers just didn't care. They told them they didn't give a damn what they did with their lives so long as they stayed away from the house. I couldn't believe their attitude, their lack of concern.

Overpowering. Brenda (left), Gerry and Barbara get a blast of opera live, during the broadcast from Sicily (May 1990).

I phoned the show and told them I wanted to change my story that day. The girls were willing to go on air. The glamour and glitz of the party would have to go on without me. As a result of the report a huge discussion on truancy and the attitudes of parents developed on the programme that morning.

That's the beauty of the show. It twists and turns according to what is happening all around it. There may be a selection of items arranged for any day's show but if something so real and instant is taking place then room can always be made for it on *The Ryan Show.*

'Look out, Brenda!'

'Look out, Brenda!' the sewer guide roared. My head bumped into a small steel girder running through the concrete. I could do nothing to stop my helmet falling off and down into the river of excrement below.

Splosh. The shock made me jerk my head up quickly. I hit the ceiling with a thud.

'Ow!' I felt like I'd been hit by a brick. I closed my eyes tight as a shot of pain sliced through my head. I kept them closed. Hopefully, when I opened them I wouldn't see the insides of a sewer.

'Owwwww!' Something wet and cold was running through my hair. I felt a terrible, slimy sensation, as if someone had cracked an egg and let the yolk slip into my scalp. The stuff, whatever it was, dripped on to my cheeks.

'Am I bleeding?' I asked.

'No. Heh. No, you're not bleeding,' came the reply.

The slime ran down my face on to my overalls. Despite the precautions I was still covered in shit and there was nothing I could do about it.

99

'I think we'd better turn back,' I said.

'Yeah,' he shrugged. 'I think you've seen enough, anyway.'

I ran my hands through my hair to pull the strands back from my face. What had I let loose from the wall; what avalanche had I caused and would I ever smell normal again?

I'd done some strange things in my career on the show, some frightening things. There was the time I had to be rescued from a ledge of a cliff, live. I talked on the air as they lifted me out into the air, on a stretcher, and winched me down to the ground. But being covered in shit in a sewer below the streets of Dublin has got to be the worst moment I've ever had on the programme.

We trudged our way back through the darkness. My guide did his best to comfort me. He wiped the slop off my hair and carried my helmet. Somehow the tape recorder survived the avalanche.

I've only myself to blame. I like to go to the whole hog when it comes to setting up an item for the programme. There's no point in presenting half the story. If it's worth doing then it's worth doing well. So if somebody

Brenda leaving RTE's side gate on her blind walk-about.

rings me up and says they get hassled when they bring their baby buggy into shops in town then I take a buggy and see what sort of reaction I get. I've spent days in everything from a woman's refuge to a fire station seeing how other people live.

Late in 1989 I suggested living with a family of travellers for a week. I'll never forget it. Instead of just doing yet another story

100

on the plight of the travelling community I wanted to see their lives up close.

Living with a family of travellers

I stayed with a family called the Powers at an unofficial halting site in Blanchardstown. Conditions were very cramped. The mother had four children. The youngest was one month old. It was naked and crying, and this was November. When I asked could I dress the child I was handed a filthy dishcloth. That wasn't to wash the child. That was to dress it. The other kids ate coal, they were so hungry. I slept in their caravan. I never got any sleep. There was a hole in the wall of the home and one night a rat crept in and ran across my blanket. I had never experienced such destitute living conditions.

My brief stay with the travellers completely changed my attitude towards them. They are a difficult group to want to understand. They have their own rules, their own world. And when their world and ours meet there is always tension and fighting. But it's impossible to forget the sight of that one-month-old baby dressed in a dirty dishcloth.

Of course, Gerry lets you express your own opinions and emotions on the subjects as well. They're not just cold, factual reports. He's very quick to notice if there's even a hint of emotion in the voice. You don't even have to tell him. He just allows the time and the space to get your feelings across.

But sometimes I must admit those emotions do get in the way. And sometimes they get you into trouble.

In June 1990 the country was running on some pretty high emotions, all right. We were slap bang in the middle of the World Cup and all Irish eyes were focused on Genoa in Italy where Ireland were due to play Romania. I was to report on the build-up to the match and, if things went well on the night, to report on the party atmosphere the day after.

I guess I let the party atmosphere get to me.

The day after the match, with little or no sleep and the memories of a night full of wild celebrations for Ireland, with traffic jams the length of the city and thousands of fans punching the night sky with pure joy, I took a cab to follow the team to Genoa airport. Somehow I managed to grab Niall Quinn for a few words with Gerry on the phone to the show. The report gave people at home a flavour of the celebrations.

'Okay, Brenda. Well done. When is your flight home?' Gerry asked me.

'Eh, well, eh, I'm not so sure. But I should be leaving soon,' I bluffed my way through the reply. By then my mind was made

The Ryan Show team and Sicilian colleagues inside the World Cup Stadium at Palermo, Sicily (May 1990).

up. I wasn't going home. They could hang me for this but I was staying where the action was. The answer from home that afternoon was 'No'. I had to come home. I had no money left and I wasn't getting any more. I phoned again and pleaded. But still the answer was 'No'.

'But *please.* I can't come home now. This is where the story is.' I was prepared to busk on the streets. I wasn't a Billy Barry kid for nothing, you know.

I can't come home now

But my constant pleading and sobbing voice eventually got the better of them. I travelled to Rome to see Ireland play Italy. I slept in a hotel room with fifty Irish lads. I ate next to nothing. And I still got a lot of grief from my producer when I got back. But it was all worth it just to be there with a lot of other Irish fans who had refused their bosses' calls to come home.

Fresh air. Oh God, I thought I'd never taste fresh air in my lungs again. I had made it to the surface, with a little bit of help from my guide, who had to push me up the steps. I sat down by the manhole for a couple of minutes while the traffic roared past. It felt good to be back on planet earth.

'I suppose you won't need to go back down for a second look?' the guide giggled. I just laughed as I drank in the air. I squeezed myself back out of the overalls. The stench wouldn't let go. It had seeped clear through to my skin. I could smell it off every single part of me. And it wouldn't disappear for a couple of weeks. All I could think of was taking a long, hot bath for about a fortnight. I needed a drink but I didn't dare go into a bar for fear of causing a riot.

Fresh air   I touched my hair with my bare hands. I felt like a walking science project. It was quite possible that somebody could have poured the entire contents of their stomach on top of me and I would have shrugged it off as a tiny mishap.

Time to go. I thanked my guide. He patted me on the back and said I wasn't the worst. He had brought some very shaky people down there and they couldn't take it for longer than sixty seconds. I had been down there for an hour.

'An hour in a sewer? Well, I suppose I can add that to my list.'

Barbara...

The Gerry Ryan Show – a by-word for fearless investigative journalism. No subject is too hot to handle, no topic too low to avoid. This morning's topic is inner city crime – or more specifically the staggering rate of larceny of bicycles in Dublin.

Whao better way to investigate crime than the good old FBI method of entrapment. I and my fearless sidekick, Private Eye Dick, set up an irresistible trap for a bike thief: a juicy red-hot 10-speed men's racing bicycle, left unlocked and unattended at railings in Stephen's Green while Dick and I watched from inside a nearby skip.

A carefully planned pincer movement Dick – an ex-Special Branch man himself, and no stranger to the high-rolling criminal godfathers of the bicycle theft underworld – assured me that we wouldn't be waiting long. He was right. My suspicious eye fell on a shifty-looking character who had been walking up and down the street for a few minutes. Suddenly he made a move for the bike. We had hit the jackpot! All pandemonium broke loose as Dick and I burst out of our hidey-hole in a carefully planned pincer movement.

'Stop, you bounder!' bellowed Dick to the disappearing thief, his long gabardine raincoat flapping in the wind, while I

Mothers

Tired of being a mother? That's what Gerry asked in the spring of 1990. Not surprisingly there were calls from exhausted women all around the country. Most of them were knackered and deserving of a couple of days off. But only one could be chosen from amongst the bunch for what turned out to be a highly publicised *Ryan Show* experiment.

Barbara Jordan, not shy herself of a bit of hard work, offered to take a mother's place for two days to see if she could survive the strain. Being single and having no kids of her own meant she was going to be at a slight disadvantage. But she'd been on survival courses before. She reckoned she could hack it for a couple of days. No problem.

The chosen mother, however, knew different.

Angela Keane had eight children. Enough for any caring, patient human being. But there was more. She also looked after another four children from the neighbourhood every day. So when Barbara took control she had a few slight adjustments to make to her life. And she had to adjust damn quick.

'Gerry,' she moaned. 'Woe is me.' Angela had left Barbara to fend for herself while she took a well-earned holiday to pamper herself with hairdressers, clothes shops, movies and dining out. By the time of her first call to the show one battalion of kids had been packed off to school. But that still left the reserves to look after.

screamed down my mobile phone to get Gerry on the line. This was it: action as it happens on the streets of Ireland.

I had carefully planned a series of Roger Cook-style questions to shout at the thief, such as, 'How many bikes a day do you nick' and 'What's the bike ever done to you'. Unfortunately, in the heat of the moment the mobile phone didn't work. Or at least, it didn't seem to be working. And, not realising the fact that the instrument had suddenly come back to life and that I was in fact through to Gerry, live on air, I screamed at the top of my voice for all the country to hear: 'Oh bollocks! This fucking phone is fucked!'

God, I hate dial tones

Ah yes, the power of modern technology, good enough to get you to the moon and back, bad enough to make an meagre human such as I sound like a complete dingbat. God, I hate dial tones.

Dicky telephones brought another potentially classic moment in Irish broadcasting to a sticky end. And that was the Great Dublin to Galway Hitch-hiking Race. Designed by humans. Destroyed by the phone. The participants: arch-rival

Brenda Donohue and myself. The challenge: to get to Galway by 12 o'clock using only the power of the thumb. The glittering prize: a weekend for two in sun-drenched Galway and about fifty quid to spend. No trick was too low, or stratagem too outrageous, to beat Donohue at this one.

You got legs – use 'em

My plan was simple. When Gerry fired the starting gun at 9 a.m., did I rush out to flag down traffic on the N4? Not bloody likely. Down with me to RTE's costumes and make-up department for a flaming red micro miniskirt and a bubbly blonde wig. Then off I went to show a little more than a talent for reporting. You got legs – use 'em.

'This'll knock 'em dead,' I thought, and I was right. My first lift arrived within seconds. So while Donohue was mournfully munching a cream bun on a Lucan roadside, I was already cheerfully whizzing past Harry's Bar in Kinnegad.

But, alas, I was to become a victim of my own success. As the twelve bells loomed, I had crossed the Galway county line and was hurtling towards the City of the Tribes,

Barbara plays mother to 12 at breakfast.

Mothers cont........

'I've only five of them left at this stage. I've been going since 7 a.m. There was a fight at the table to see who would get the free toy in the cornflakes box so there's sugar and milk all over the floor. Then the milk was spilt on their homework. So I had to write a note to the teacher excusing the kids.' She was being continually interrupted by her new family as she talked to Gerry.

'Oh, and I've got to stop Danielle from ripping the wallpaper and writing on the wall with a big green pen.'

While Angela would normally have the washing done by the middle of the day, Barbara was still wrestling with the kids, trying to keep them occupied.

Her life depended on her cooking. If she didn't have a tray of fairy cakes ready for them after school she'd be murdered. She put the call out for a recipe for the cakes. Sure enough, she had her instructions from a listener within minutes. It was clear somebody was having sympathy for the new mother. Her life was saved, for the moment.

By the second day, Barbara was a wreck. She had been working for almost all the past twenty-four hours. When Gerry rang her she couldn't come to the phone, she was that busy. So Nicola told Gerry what she thought of Barbara's housework. 'Well, she's good at playing games and she's good at making apple crumble. She's not bad at ironing either.'

'What are the bad things, then?'

'Well, dinner wasn't so good last night. She hadn't cooked the chicken properly. There were a few tummy aches. Then there were no fairy cakes for school this morning.'

Barbara came on the phone to give her side of the gruelling story.

'Barbara, I believe they're calling you Big Knickers.'

'That's not all, Gerry. They're also calling me Big Fat Bra-Bra. The only time they've been affectionate over the last twenty-four hours was when it came to bedtime last night and they wanted to stay up. They were making me cups of tea and cleaning the kitchen. Of course, they got to stay up late. I'd been on my feet for fifteen hours at that stage. I could have done with the help.' She admitted she was well shagged out.

'I feel like I've got a multiple hangover and all I've been doing is minding kids. I got three and a half hours' sleep last night. The real mammy and daddy didn't come home last night. They had a great meal in a local hotel restaurant and then they were invited to stay the night in the place. So I had to look after the army. One of the children likes to bang his head

courtesy of a friendly woman driver who found space for me between her two kids in the back seat. Unfortunately we had entered The Land That Mobile Phones Forgot, one of the danger zones for radio journalists where the air signal is too weak and the bloody things don't work. My phone was dead, and, to add insult to injury, I could hear on the car radio that Donohue had the audacity to ring in from somewhere near Athlone claiming victory.

'As it is now 1 minute to 12 and there is no sign of Jordan, I must now declare you the winner of the Great B and B Race to Galway,' said Gerry to Brenda, on the air. It was official.

I shrieked at this outrageous miscarriage of justice. I refused to accept defeat and to forfeit the prize which geographically was now mine. I burst out of the car and into a public phone box. Would I make it? Who could forget the nailbiting end to 'Around the World in 80 Days', when just at the stroke of noon Fogg arrived at the Reform Club in London? Was I to achieve a similar triumph?

Not today, Barbara. The Angelus sounded and DJ

Colm Hayes came on air. When I did get through I asked to announce my victory to the nation. But instead of congratulation and support I was told to bugger off. I was too late. The chalice of glory had slipped from my lips, for that day at any rate.

One question I am very often asked is, 'Don't you have a great life going to foreign countries and all?' I do my best to be kind to these poor specimens, and I normally say 'No, not at

Mothers cont........

off the headboard. He does this regularly. I thought his head was going to be done in but I've been told the bone in his head has adapted to take this banging into account.

'I feel I've done a complete peace-keeping role better than anything the United Nations has ever done.'

Barbara had a major re-think about the joys of parenthood when she finally made it back to the office. She put her motherly skills to one side. But the supreme title of 'Big Knickers' has tagged along ever since.

'It sounds like I'm moaning, but this is what women are doing every day.'

all'. Take my trip to India, for example, culminating as it did with my visit to the historic Taj Mahal.

India! Great Continent, Empire, Nation, Republic. Magnificent land of many cultures, peoples and religions. Culinary India with its exotic rice, fish and meat dishes. Historic India, with its temples and shrines. A land of contrasts, great wealth co-existing with great poverty. A natural wonderland of mountain ranges and shimmering blue seas. Exotic wildlife, vultures, elephants, tigers, crocodiles. This was the India I came to see, the images that drew me to the great subcontinent.

These were some of the images of which I saw nothing or next to nothing.

Two of the family of 12 Barbara had to look after.

Almost all of my time was spent in uninteresting hotel rooms trying to make phone calls to Dublin. The Indian phone system – now there's an exotic wonder of the world. Once again a technological masterpiece that forgot about the humans using it.

Day after day I spent trying to get a line to Montrose. It became an obsession. How could I go out and see India if I couldn't relate my tales to the people of Ireland? After all, this wasn't some kind of leisurely report: 'Well, Gerry, thanks for the spending money, I had a great time in India.' This was live radio, vigorous, thrusting, fresh and exciting. Taped reports are for yesterday's media. Ryan is happening, hip-hop, here and now. If I couldn't get through to Dublin on a clear line the whole thing was a waste of time. Eventually a few calls did get through, but the whole exercise made me sweat blood and cry into my pillow.

I should have been a lumberjack

The supposed climax to the trip was a visit to the Taj Mahal, which is at its best at sunset. Then the sun's rays strike the alabaster palace walls creating a dazzling spectacle of marble and light, which, as I can personally declare, is literally unforgettable. Truly a wonder of the world. Delayed by another failed phone call, I arrived at the Taj Mahal in pitch darkness. I could see nothing. Someone held up a cigarette lighter to help me make out the building. What a total disaster. I should have been a lumberjack.

On one of my travels around the four green fields I went to Enniscrone in County Sligo to discover what the modern woman takes to her bath. You'd be amazed to find out exactly what the women of Ireland like to use to soothe those aches and pains. For some, it's another body, for others, it's a good old bubble bath. But for me, one morning, it was a big, slobbery, slimy mass of seaweed.

Ensconced in the Edwardian splen-

A vegetable stew

dour of the Enniscrone Seaweed Baths, I gently lowered myself into a steaming enamel cauldron of oceanic plant life. I felt like an ingredient in a vegetable stew simmering on a hot plate. The seaweed was freshly harvested that morning and, tossed into the bath, it came alive, as it were, in a riot of colour.

'It's an incredible sight,' I explained to Gerry while I studied the slimy surroundings.

'I'd say it is, all right,' Gerry replied. Well, what was I to expect.

It glowed red and orange and emitted a strange, gooey, oily substance as it massaged my body. To my great surprise, what

110

seemed like a horrible mushy mass of organic tripe turned out to be a sensual delight.

'But is it not going up to your bum, Barbara?' said Gerry.

That wasn't the point.

'Then where's it going? It must be going somewhere. Are you ticklish? Is it moving? Is there anybody in there with you?'

Part-time broadcaster, full-time housewife Siobhain Hough tries on a pair of 'seaweed socks' during the show.

Sligo is surprising! Sligo yielded up more of its secrets to me a few months later when I got a call to investigate a strange sighting on Dunmoran Strand. The RTE switchboard was plagued with calls about a strange figure who stalked the early morning strand, dressed in full Alpine regalia, complete with ski boots, skis, a fur-lined adventure sports jacket and sun visor.

Who is this man, I asked myself. Is he some Alpine castaway, sole survivor of a shipwreck, or just an escaped mental patient? Or could he have been brought to our shores by timewarp, like Dr Who? Maybe he was a tourist promotion. After all, the region's tourist slogan declares that Sligo is surprising!

He was none of these things. Fred Zesserson, a diminutive, former radical Wall Street lawyer, turned journalist, publisher and publicist, came from a flourishing practice at the bar in the State of New York to make a home in Ireland, attracted by the peace and tranquillity of lovely Sligo.

'Fred,' I said, 'What's with the ski gear?'

'It's a great new sport: sand skiing,' he enthused. I was utterly unconvinced. Never having skied before, my perception was that gravity played an important role in proceedings. Staring out at the dead level sands of Dunmoran, I was fortified in my belief that old Fred was, to say the least, taking the mickey.

A great new sport

'You're having me on,' I said.

'No no, come see for yourself.' So I came and saw for myself. To my amazement Fred had assembled a crack squad of local skiers, each one ready, stick in hand, to do battle with the sand and the elements.

'Okay, GO!' said Fred. And suddenly the skiers shot across the surface of the beach, arms pumping their ski sticks. The skis moved like gliders along the sand. Fred's long hours of practice came good and his lithe, tanned 69-year-old figure was the first to cross the finishing line. The skiers were a marvel to

'Is this some Irish joke?'

behold. I could only stand back and say to myself: it's a funny old world.

Gerry refused to believe it. He said it was an Irish joke and that I was pulling his leg. He should talk about pulling legs. I had meant to take a photograph of the scene on the beach but my camera wouldn't work. I'm beginning to think I'm jinxed.

Unlike some other great media institutions, *The Gerry Ryan Show* does not revolve around objective, impartial, unemotional reporting. But sometimes the events that Brenda and I cover can tug unexpectedly at the heartstrings.

I remember one morning I was dispatched to the Dublin Society for the Prevention of Cruelty to Animals to investigate a report that fifty dogs were put down in the capital every day. A staff member showed me around, but the clean, tidy, almost

Forty Foot ....

It began with a phone call. It ended with a splash. And the waves Mary Downes created rippled as far across the globe as Japan.

All she did was phone the show one day and tell Gerry she was going to take her clothes off and the more people who saw her in the act the better. As it turned out, a crowd of 600 people, most of them waving cameras in her direction, attended her well-publicised unwrapping down on the rocks off Dublin Bay. She was going for a dip in the nip. And she wanted everyone to know why.

A week before the event Mary Downes, a young woman from Balbriggan, rang *The Gerry Ryan Show* to tell him about the day she went for a swim in the Forty Foot. Lying at the foot of James Joyce's tower on the coast at Sandycove, the rocky bathing spot has for over a hundred years been the location for a male-only nude swimmers' club.

'I've been there a few times, Gerry,' said Mary, as she explained what happened. 'But yesterday I went there with my boyfriend. I was the only woman there. I mean, I knew there were going to be naked men there. But I wasn't bothered by it.

'But what I found were thirty pairs of eyes wanting me, willing me, to get out of the place. My boyfriend actually noticed it before I did. But I decided I wasn't going to be intimidated. I decided to leave but I told them that I'd be back.

'I thought, there and then, I'd ring you and rally as many women as possible to go there, next Monday morning.'

Gerry's eyes lit up. There's nothing like a confrontation to stir the stew.

'So,' he said. 'You want as many women as possible to take their clothes off down at the Forty Foot next Monday, do you?'

'I said I'd be back with twenty naked women. They said fine. I just want to teach them a lesson. And I'll start it. I just want to be able to go down to the Forty Foot and swim.'

She'd made her point. She sounded like a determined woman in her own quiet way, out to prove something without bringing down the wrath of women everywhere.

More than a decade earlier a group of women, including Nell McCafferty, made the headlines by invading the traditional male hideaway down at the Forty Foot. But this time it was not a principle at stake. It was simply the right for anyone to go swimming, anywhere.

Calls of support began rolling in as soon as 'Downsey' finished talking on the air. The calls didn't all come from women. One man said he'd

Forty Foot cont........

provide buses to transport supporters. Another caller phoned in to say he had a little business on the side.

'We sell ice cream from a golf caddy, Gerry. A friend of mine has adapted an old buggy for the job. So he wonders could he have permission from yourself to be the official seller?'

'Well I'm not too sure, really. Like I've been saying, it *is* about making a point about being able to swim.'

'I'm sure we could come to some sort of arrangement. You know ... cut you in, like. Perhaps we might be able to slip a brown envelope your way, know what I mean?'

'Oh yes, oh absolutely. Yes, you have my permission. Just make sure the envelope is delivered directly to me, now. Don't give it to anyone else. Okay?'

'Okay then, Gerry. And how about selling buckets and spades for the kiddies like ... '

In the week that followed the calls came in as if this was the last chance for a summer beach party. Buses were coming from all over the country. Barbara Jordan was asked to do a special report from the Forty Foot on the day. There was an offer of security for Downsey and her nude supporters which they accepted. They were going to need it.

And even though the storming of the Forty Foot was nothing new, the newspapers picked up on it and ran reports of Downsey's plan. After all, this was the silly season, the time when, traditionally, there is little or no news to report. And anyhow, most people preferred to be out in the sun. So, to give the summer a helping hand the media always love to print a good silly story or two. And what

sterile environment could not hide the grisly work that went on there. For the vet, it was just another day's work. As he prepared his equipment we chatted about the irresponsibility of some dog owners. We decided to do a dry run before I went on air.

First on the death list was a massive 7-year-old German shepherd. The dog was in perfect health and had a docile, affable nature for its breed. His owners had left him in the previous day to be put down because they were having a baby.

The dog trusted us all and jumped obediently on to the table. When the vet produced the needle he got a little suspicious and cowered away. He did his best to pull his paw away from the lethal injection but, in a matter of seconds, he was dead.

I burst out crying

Much to everyone's shock I burst out crying. I phoned the office to say I couldn't go on. I couldn't bear it. But as always, there was some delay before I was supposed to go on air. I had time then to compose myself and, after a cup of tea, I took the plunge and phoned back to talk the nation through the killing of a bull terrier. I faltered a bit, but my eyes stayed dry. Gerry sensed I was beginning to get upset again. He made it easier for me by cutting short the story after the dog had been destroyed.

I know Brenda and I go to great pains to get a good story. But one rather painful story taught me a lot about exactly how far I should go for the show.

One morning I took myself off to a beauty parlour in the city centre to spend the morning in the hands of a beautician who wooed me with the promise of making me feel better about my appearance by artificially interfering with it.

Aladdin's Cave

The beauty parlour was like an Aladdin's Cave, or Santa's Den. Full of busy, ordered activity: eyelashes were being dyed, nails manicured, eyebrows plucked, faces massaged. But like the raw reporter that I was, I signed up for the worst experience of all: the bikini line treatment.

Barbara and Brenda speed off to track down another story - this time it's Sicily !

I must have been bonkers, is all that I cay say. How could I let her near such a sensitive part of the body. The pain, discomfort and subsequent bruising left me in no doubt that beauty is not something you can create in a one-hour session. Of course, being older and wiser now I have learned how to better story than one with plenty of pictures. Apart from being a stand for the freedom of the swimmer this was going to be a picture editor's dream: nudity making the news.

'I don't see why she should be freaking out over this,' one male swimmer told Gerry. 'If she swam there regularly she'd see that all the naked swimmers were over seventy years of age. There are no young guys letting it all hang out. And they also supply their own lifeguards.' But the argument continued to grow between those who wished to preserve the male nude bathing spot and those who wished to break it down.

On Friday, three days before the dip, *The Gerry Ryan Show* broadcast from a studio in Paris. It was 14 July, France's Independence Day and their bi-centennial year. Gerry and the team reported on the excitement and celebration in the streets while Terence tried to make a speech from the studio window. But not even the freedom of one country could be celebrated fully without the story of the freedom of the individual in the Forty Foot. While Paris went wild on the streets, Downsey and a representative of the all-male bathers' association at Sandycove went for each other's throats on the telephone lines.

'I don't give a damn about naked men,' said Downsey. 'The fact that they're breaking a rule is not the issue. It's the fact that when a woman goes down to the Forty Foot they don't want her there,' she argued.

'For her to say she couldn't swim there, she is a liar,' said the man. 'I can produce fifty women who swim there.' And that wasn't the end of his

Barbara with Mary Downes, 'Downsey', after her 'Dip in the Nip' in the Forty Foot.

116

Forty Foot cont........

attack. He went on to reveal how Downsey was the lead singer with a rock group.

'I regard you as a twenty-year-old brat looking for publicity. You're a publicity-seeking hound. You're a failed rock singer,' he roared.

'At twenty years of age?'

Gerry looked at the producer. There was nothing they could do as the two went to war over the air.

'I didn't want anybody to know I was in a band. I'm not looking for publicity for a band. I'm not even gigging with a band. It no longer exists.'

'When the sun comes out every dingbat and flasher comes out too, including your friend here,' the man explained to Gerry.

The more they argued the more people booked their seats on one of the rocks overlooking the tiny inlet of water that was about to become the focus of attention throughout the country, and beyond.

What rolled into view for Barbara and producer Willy O'Reilly as they arrived in Sandycove the following Monday morning made them freeze in the sun. A traffic jam of buses, cars, police and vendors slowly wormed its way to the Forty Foot. It could have been a concert taking place, except there was no band in sight.

The only music to be heard was the tune being played on Gerry's show, amplified and booming out around the area from a hundred radios and ghettoblasters. The sun bore down on the bodies. There was a party mood in the air. It was plain to see this was one of the most publicised showdowns, but the place was so full no one could tell the spectators from the bathers' association.

Barbara and Willy squeezed their way through the crowd of onlookers. The police kept an eye on the huge numbers on the rocks. Out on the water an inflatable boat with scuba-divers on board patrolled the coast. The heat of the sun made conditions all the more uncomfortable. The only vantage point offering any cool relief was the sea itself.

Barbara inched her way as close to the water's edge as she could without making her own splashing statement. She tried to phone the studio on her mobile phone but the crush of bodies all around her was blocking the signal. The only way to broadcast, then, was from above the crowd. They climbed up on one of the rocks overlooking the scene and waited then for the most celebrated dip in the nip to take place.

The Forty Foot had never seen crowds like this before. Nor had it attracted so many pairs of ears to its location as hundreds of thousands tuned into the show.

Then from out of the wriggling rows of onlookers came Downsey. She was accompanied by some supporters and security who eased her through the crowd. She looked like a boxer about to step in to the ring to disrobe and do battle. The crowd roared with approval as she made her way to the edge of the steps in to the water.

The cameras whirred and clicked as spectators snapped their memories and press men got their shot. Up on the ledge Barbara's signal worked and, a little shakily from her high vantage point, she described to listeners the action down below her.

Downsey slipped out of her robe. The crowd roared in support. The heat was on and people wanted flesh. She wore a bikini bottom, and top. She waved to the crowd and dived into the cold water. As she bobbed up and down in the swell she reached for the clip at the back of her bikini top and took it off, waving it to her audience who applauded her individual stance. But others roared for 'more'.

'There were about 500 people crammed on to those rocks out there,' Willy recalled. 'I was standing, perched on a rock right next to Barbara. Then the next thing, as Downsey is swimming around, four women next to me whipped off their clothes and dived in with her. The whole scene was wild.'

A blow for individuality. A story to warm the hearts and a spread of naked flesh that ran in all the national newspapers the next day, and in one city paper as far away as Japan. In an interview in one paper a few days after the event Downsey said she felt great about what she had done. She explained how for some days after the event she was congratulated by people of both sexes.

The day after her dip she returned to the Forty Foot. All the excitement and noise had long gone home. There were only a handful of people down by the rocks, including some women. She went swimming without raising an eyelid from any bather, either male or female . . . .

give Gerry a graphic description of events without subjecting myself to the full frontal experience, only part of it.

But there have still been occasional genuine stomach-churning moments. The morning I had to deliver a lamb, on air, was pretty disgusting. I had to stick my hand up the mother to ease out the little lamb, covered in indescribable gooey fluids. And with the other hand I had to talk to Gerry by mobile phone.

Once the poor creature had arrived into this world, unaware that it was an instant star of a radio show, I had to hold its hind legs and spin it around to bring it to its senses. I felt like an Olympic hammer thrower, but I had to resist the temptation of letting go the lamb.

And if putting my hand in mysterious places gets me brownie points, then I'll never ever forget the day I had to put my hand into a bucket of animal innards. I was on a treasure hunt. To get one clue I had to plunge my hand into a bucket of offal. There I was, up to my elbow in pigs' blood looking for some stupid message while a crowd of people looked on and smiled as if I was a kid dipping into a lucky bag. If the dog execution was the nearest I came to crying on air, the offal bucket was the nearest I came to puking. The smell lingered on my skin for weeks after. I could not even look at meat for a month.

Groovy Greta

'Well, Brenda, or, should I say, Groovy Greta. It seems that your truck is the first to reach the Unifreight Depot in the Great G. Ryan Show Continental Trucking Race.'

'That's right, Gerry. Looks like I'm the winner!'

Oh no. Not again.

Delighted and excited, Brenda burst into song.

'I like trucking, I like trucking . . . and I like to truck.'

On the road again! Brenda, Gerry and Barbara prior to embarking on the 'Mars/ Gerry Ryan Show Italy or Bust' journey to Sicily.

Kitten Kate

'Are you going to bring Kitten Kate with you on this magnificent trip to Paris which you've just won?' Gerry asked mischievously.

'Not on your life, Gerry. That bucket-mass deserves to lose. You know what they say – the winner takes it all.'

While Brenda, alias Groovy Greta, was gloating on air, my truck was stuck at red lights in Phibsboro. Utterly defeated, again, I phoned Gerry to take it on the chin. My spirits were lifted momentarily when Gerry offered his commiserations and said that a glittering second prize awaited me at the depot. I cracked the whip and Sean Heffernan, my truck driver, put his foot to the floor.

When we reached the depot I jumped out eagerly, thinking of a bottle of Dom Perignon and a diamond necklace. Imagine my

119

surprise when I was presented with a bucket and mop and told that I had the honour of cleaning Unifreight's fleet of enormous juggernauts.

'That's not a consolation prize, Gerry. That's penal servitude,' I said indignantly.

'This is nothing to do with penises. Now grab your brush and go.'

Hair grooming session for 9 of the 12 kids Barbara was to be mother to for a few days in May 1990.

Hectic and hilarious   The trucking race was hectic and hilarious from start to finish. Brenda and I played the role of CB Queens, Groovy Greta and Kitten Kate. So our reports were punctuated by CB lingo, which meant there was a lot of 'Breaker Breaker', 'Smokey Bears' and 'Big Ten Fours'. Officially the race had started on a Sunday when we had both left the North Wall on the same ferry. The haulage company had supplied the trucks as well as our drivers, Johnny McEvoy and Sean Heffernan.

By Monday morning both trucks were rattling along the British motorway system, vying with each other to get to Dover for the next ferry crossing. Still neck and neck at Calais, we went our separate ways. Brenda and Johnny had to drop their load in Germany while Sean and myself were heading for a warehouse in Brussels.

The rules of the game were that we had to drop our loads successfully and then wait for instructions from home as to where we had to pick up our return batch of goods. Both trucks *had* to go home with capacity loads.

As usual, Brenda was luckier. Probably because she bribed somebody. She quickly got word of a full load to be picked up in a German village, close to where they had made their drop. My news was not so good. Sean and I would have to go to three different European countries to fill up the truck.

Developments and updates on the race were coloured with our observations about the world of trucking and their fraternity. For Brenda and me this was a totally new way of life. Okay, so we spend a lot of time travelling. But sleeping in the cabs of these giant trucks was a completely new thing. For the truckers, however, their life was as ordered and routine as that of an office job.

Hanging out – this time in the proper place, Barbara washing for 12.

People still ask us about the events of that unforgettable week and, nine times out of ten, the question on everyone's lips is: 'Which one of you hung their knickers out on the wing mirror of the truck?' And, of course, I always say I can't remember.

My visit to Romania in November 1990 was certainly the worst ordeal of my career with the programme.

Romania From beginning to end the trip was fraught with difficulties, which started with my application to travel from the RTE Authority. The application was turned down because it was considered too expensive. For a time it seemed the plan had fallen foul of the ferocious cutbacks brought about by the onslaught of independent broadcasting.

However, this time the producers decided to fight the decision. They felt strongly that we should send a reporter to Romania, if only to lend continuity to the huge public reaction and interest that had been provoked by the original stories of abuse and neglect of the orphans of Romania.

Eventually permission to travel was granted. But not without first getting sponsorship from a baby food manufacturer.

The first orphanage I visited in Romania was one of the recently adopted Irish concerns, situated seventy miles from Bucharest in the suburbs of a town called Videle. At that time the Comber orphanage appeal had only just sent in a team of voluntary workers; their brief was to make structural changes and improvements to the building, which did not have electricity, plumbing or sewage.

I was warned that I would find the children and the building in a raw state. While the orphanage was being made fit for habitation, the Irish medical staff were commuting every day from Bucharest in the back of an old Transit van that reeked of Romanian rationed diesel. We sang songs in the back of the van to keep the motion sickness at bay. I wondered what lay ahead of me.

Two hours later the van swerved to the right on to an old dirt track that led to the orphanage. The workmen from Northern Ireland gathered around outside to give a warm welcome. It occurred to me that things could not be all that bad as the men appeared relaxed and good humoured. They suggested a cup of tea inside, so we all traipsed gratefully after them, up the broken concrete steps that met the battered entrance door with its broken glass and jail bars.

As soon as we crossed the **Broken glass and jail bars** threshold all my senses were assaulted. Straightaway we were surrounded by naked teenagers with shaved heads and gaping infected wounds. They tugged aggressively at our clothes and made disturbing grunting noises. Hefty women in hospital blue dresses intervened, slapping them from our sides. They didn't seem to notice the force with which they had been hit.

They followed us down a semi-dark corridor which had open doorways revealing groups of younger children, mainly small babies and toddlers. Some were alone in metal cots, others had been herded together on to filthy blankets laid on the stone floor. Bodies were mutilated by strange bone deformities. Small, pained faces, with saucer brown eyes, begged an explanation as they told a tale of lovelessness and brutality.

Small, pained faces The atmosphere was redolent of vomit, ammonia, excrement and a vile humid cooking smell. By the time we reached the end of the corridor where the men had established makeshift living quarters I could feel the nausea rising. Quickly I turned on my heels and made it as far as the main entrance where I got sick on the steps.

122

Barbara and company singing songs from 'Grease' during an outside broadcast, January 1991.

Throughout my stay in Romania feelings of nausea were never too far away. The orphanages are not the only monster created by the worst excesses of communism. Everywhere there is evidence of the damage caused by a cruel, calculated experiment. People talked openly of how they felt psychologically molested and desensitised, and of how their spirit had been crushed by corruption and nine-hour milk queues.

Altogether I visited eight of the estimated 250 State orphanages in Romania. Each one **Savage neglect** presented similar scenes of malnutrition, brutality and savage neglect.

My reports from Romania were sent, live, from the National Broadcasting Centre in Bucharest and were definitely the most difficult live broadcasts I have ever had to do. I knew that I was extremely raw, emotionally, and felt worried that I would not be capable of conveying the misery and privation I had witnessed. Unsure of myself, I sat in front of a studio microphone and went on air to talk about abandoned children in concentration camps.

It was not easy. My upset was very obvious to anyone listening. But thankfully I managed to remain coherent, none the less. I was glad to get home. I can't say Ireland's a bed of roses or anything, but at least here there is a freedom.

123

Mickey Joe...

'Okay, good luck now, Gerry.' These were the immortal words that sparked off one of the most sensational sagas ever to hold the attention of the *Gerry Ryan Show* audience.

Going underground for every farmer in the country

Those parting words were from the voice of farmer Mickey Joe Brady as he left this world for the confined space of a coffin that was to be his home, six feet underground, for many months to come.

The story began two days before that, in August 1990. Gerry was on his first day back in the studio after his holidays. A caller had just rung the show to tell him he saw a naked woman driving a car through Tralee. It looked as if things were back to normal. Then a man called Pat Breslin rang the studio and asked to speak to Gerry. He had a very special story for him, an offer the show could not refuse.

He said he had a friend who had a few points to make about the plight of the small farmer in Ireland. But he wasn't going to just talk. He was going to do something about it. And he asked Gerry would the show be interested in covering the story as it unfolded.

Pat's friend was Mickey Joe Brady. He was preparing to break the world burial record which had been set at 141 days. Mickey Joe would spend the next five months living in a coffin six feet underground. And instead of taking all the risks for his own publicity he was going underground for every farmer in the country. At the time the United States was putting pressure on the European Community to cut subsidies to the small farmer. Mickey Joe wanted everyone to know that this move would surely bury the small Irish farmer, for good. And he was about to put some action behind those stirring words.

On 22 August 1990 Barbara Jordan attended the official 'burial' of Mickey Joe Brady. One of the local farmers helped dig the hole with a bulldozer. The box was lowered down, together with its vital air tube – a tall piece of piping, measuring four inches in diameter. The box itself measured 54 cubic feet. It was six foot long and only three feet wide, according to the specifications of the current world record.

Beautiful morning for a burial

It was a clear beautiful morning for a burial. Mickey Joe was up with the dawn and took his dog Blackie for a walk through the fields. He owned a small farm of thirty-five acres. At forty years of age he should have had a growing family around him. But he never married. He led a solitary life.

Mickey Joe knew he wouldn't need to dress in style where he was going. He wore a plain one-piece boiler suit and took with him three jumpers and a sleeping bag, along with a couple of pairs of underpants.

He explained all his many preparations to Gerry only moments before he himself climbed down the steep ledge into his new home. He explained how, as a training exercise, he had gone underground in a coffin for two hours at a carnival earlier in the year. But this next phase in his life would be different.

Gerry wished him all the best.

'Okay, good luck now, Gerry,' he replied and handed the mobile phone back to Barbara. He climbed down into the coffin. Once he was lying down comfortably a package was handed down to him by Pat Breslin. In it were some books and magazines, including the Bible, *Moby Dick* and old copies of *Ireland's Own* and *The Farmers Journal*. There was also a supply of sweets donated by a company which had heard his story on the show.

Pat passed down an electric fan heater with an extension lead and a pack of black plastic bags for his waste. Then it was time to seal the coffin lid. After a couple of waves to the small group of helpers on the ground above, the lid was placed into position. A solicitor helped seal the lid by hammering the final nail in to the coffin. Then, slowly and carefully, the hired hands began the task of burying Mickey Joe alive. The nation listened as Barbara described the scene. It was a chilling moment.

A chilling moment Some time later in the same morning Gerry returned to Barbara at the scene. She described that all was now quiet. The hired hands were waiting around to see how the ground would settle. When it was considered safe Barbara walked over the soft earth to the air vent leading down to Mickey Joe. She put the phone up to the vent and asked Mickey Joe to put his radio walkman on so that he could hear Gerry talking.

'How are you, Mickey Joe?'

'Fine, fine, Gerry.' He seemed nervous as he slowly took to his new surroundings. The light from his electric bulb was dim. It was hard to make out details except for what he could see within the shaft of light from the vent.

But he knew he was not alone. He had taken a guest in with him as the lid had been slipped into place.

'There's a wee spider just after crawling across me, Gerry. I couldn't see how big it was. But at least I know I've got a friend down here with me.'

Mickey Joe cont........

From then on the show took regular reports from the burial site. Its location was always kept secret to keep onlookers away. They weren't doing this as a spectacle. After all, there was nothing to see except for a bit of piping stuck in the ground. But it was a serious event and with a message for farmers everywhere.

Calls of support and encouragement began flooding into the office. Mickey Joe had a lot of followers in just a few short weeks. His high spirits and good-natured attitude helped sustain him through the days and nights. And as the weeks wore on he developed a strong religious belief as well as a love for the music of Pavarotti.

Smell of burning One night Mickey Joe woke up to the smell of burning. He couldn't think where it was coming from. But the smell was getting stronger. He shouted out for Pat Breslin but no one heard him. He tried the intercom system that had been built into the coffin. But there was no reply. Suddenly Mickey Joe was faced with the prospect of dying in a fiery hell, only six feet from the surface.

It was then that he ordered himself to calm down, to relax and think carefully about where this burning smell might be coming from. He very quickly realised the cause. A black polythene bag had got caught in the grille of the blow heater. It had slipped in behind the grille and melted on to the element of the heater. The panic was calmly averted and Mickey Joe had learned an important fact about his life underground.

'Gerry, I thought I was a gonner for sure,' he explained on the air the following morning. 'But even in the worst moments, Gerry, you've got to summon up the help of the Almighty. He'll see you through.'

The most unusual thing that happened during the whole ordeal was when Pat Breslin lost his creamery cheque. When he was talking to Mickey Joe one morning he told his friend he could not find the cheque he had received for his milk. Miraculously, Mickey Joe told Pat to look between the cooker and the press in his kitchen. He did. The cheque was there. Mickey Joe explained that he had had an out-of-body experience and had followed Pat as he searched for the piece of paper. He had seen it quite clearly. But he could say nothing in that state and had to wait until he returned to his body.

As time wore on and the listeners became accustomed to the slight, wee voice of this man from somewhere in the north midlands, the pressure and stress of living in such confined conditions began to take their toll. Mickey Joe slipped into a depression as he grew less confident in his challenge. For some weeks he felt as if no one was listening to him and that all was in vain. But only the regular visits from Barbara seemed

Mickey Joe cont........

to help ease the strain. He felt he had a friend in Barbara, and she did all she could to make his life a happier one.

A hoax Tragedy struck when he received a letter from London telling him that his cousin had been badly injured in an accident and was on a life support machine. He was asked to give up his record attempt and come to help his relative. Like a true Christian he agreed, and decided to give up his attempt which was still six weeks away from the record. But the truth was quick to follow. On the morning he had decided to come up he received a call from his cousin in London. He had not been hurt in any accident. The letter was, in fact, a hoax. And, while the culprits were never found, it is still strongly believed the letter was contrived by a gambler who bet a fortune that Mickey Joe would not beat the record.

At Christmas *The Ryan Show* celebrated the season by broadcasting their show from a town in Switzerland. But Mickey Joe wasn't left out of the fun. He was linked up to the show in the final hour by Barbara, who at the last moment had decided to stay behind and be with the brave farmer.

There were just two weeks to go. The calls of support increased as the record time ran out. There was a rumour that one individual had bet £30,000 on Mickey Joe setting a new record. Meanwhile, the man himself was feeling stronger and happier every day.

It snowed during the last week of his burial. It was windy and bitterly cold. And on Wednesday 9 January, one day before the record was beaten, Mickey Joe woke up with a jolt at five in the morning. Something was wrong. Not far from where he was buried was a large concrete tank carrying effluent. In the icy conditions the wall had cracked. It wasn't a very big crack, but enough for the liquid to begin seeping out and trailing gently down the hill to where Mickey Joe lay.

He didn't know it then, but soon Mickey Joe's temporary home would become a growing pond of effluent. The sound of that crack was enough to send him screaming for help once more through the intercom. By the time *The Ryan Show* had kicked off on another cold January morning it was clear to the team that he was not going to make it beyond the record. But, more importantly now, was his life in danger from the threat of the effluent?

The first call came through from Pat Breslin. Out of breath and clearly upset, he explained to Gerry that a bulldozer was clearing away the muck and slime but the digging was being done by hand to prevent a possible cave-in on Mickey Joe.

More than five hours had passed since the crack in the wall had appeared. The liquid was by now seeping down into the coffin which had not been built to be watertight. Mickey Joe was shivering in the cold, damp conditions. He was screaming to get out. The record was lost. Now it was an all-out effort to save this man.

Barbara had rushed to the scene on first hearing the news. She began her reports from the scene shortly after 11 a.m. The farmers were digging with their bare hands and a water pump was brought in to reduce any chances of drowning.

The cold chilly light of January smacked Mickey Joe in the eyes as he was lifted to safety and into the arms of Barbara. He was rushed inside and covered in blankets. His ordeal was over. He was glad to be alive. And even in his close shave with death, he grabbed the first chance to talk to Gerry on air and repeat the message:

'Farmers are fighting the elements day in day out, Gerry. This is our life.'